To Sue

With loving good

Petra

Stepping Stones on the Spiritual Path

Inspirational Spiritual Writings

ASTRA FERRO

BALBOA
PRESS
A DIVISION OF HAY HOUSE

Copyright © 2017 Astra Ferro.

All rights reserved. No part of this book may be used or reproduced by any means, graphic, electronic, or mechanical, including photocopying, recording, taping or by any information storage retrieval system without the written permission of the author except in the case of brief quotations embodied in critical articles and reviews.

This book is a work of non-fiction. Unless otherwise noted, the author and the publisher make no explicit guarantees as to the accuracy of the information contained in this book and in some cases, names of people and places have been altered to protect their privacy.

Balboa Press books may be ordered through booksellers or by contacting:

Balboa Press
A Division of Hay House
1663 Liberty Drive
Bloomington, IN 47403
www.balboapress.com
1 (877) 407-4847

Because of the dynamic nature of the Internet, any web addresses or links contained in this book may have changed since publication and may no longer be valid. The views expressed in this work are solely those of the author and do not necessarily reflect the views of the publisher, and the publisher hereby disclaims any responsibility for them.

The author of this book does not dispense medical advice or prescribe the use of any technique as a form of treatment for physical, emotional, or medical problems without the advice of a physician, either directly or indirectly. The intent of the author is only to offer information of a general nature to help you in your quest for emotional and spiritual well-being. In the event you use any of the information in this book for yourself, which is your constitutional right, the author and the publisher assume no responsibility for your actions.

Any people depicted in stock imagery provided by Thinkstock are models, and such images are being used for illustrative purposes only.
Certain stock imagery © Thinkstock.

Print information available on the last page.

ISBN: 978-1-5043-7866-6 (sc)
ISBN: 978-1-5043-7868-0 (hc)
ISBN: 978-1-5043-7867-3 (e)

Library of Congress Control Number: 2017905539

Balboa Press rev. date: 04/17/2017

Dedication

I dedicate this book to my Teacher, Guide and Mentor and to the Ancestral Group Soul who have helped me over so many years. Their guidance, their patience and above all their love have been the source of my soul understanding and the force behind my own journey.

Acknowledgement

Over the years, I have read many books whose knowledge and teaching have inspired me along the path and have been instrumental in helping me to move forward along my own stepping stones.

I particularly would like to pay tribute to the Teachings of:

Master Djwhal Khul through the Alice Bailey books
White Eagle
Henry Thomas Hamblin
Joel Goldsmith

Foreword

To those who are awakening to the spiritual journey, the many writings on the subject can seem overwhelming and difficult to understand. Often writers will convey their information and spiritual insights using terminology that seems foreign and difficult to fathom. Yet in this book the author, *Astra Ferro*, has tailored her profound understanding of the spiritual dimension of life in a way that shows remarkable sensitivity to those new to the Spiritual Path.

Largely written in a question and answer format, *Stepping Stones on the Spiritual Path* provides a marvellous introduction to the soul and its evolution over time. Using her many years of study, coupled with personal experience, the author provides simple to understand principles related to recognizing the seven types of souls, reincarnation, spiritual freedom and much more. Also included are a variety of skills to be cultivated along the way.

Without reservation, I wholeheartedly recommend this book to anyone seeking to live a more soulful and meaningful life. It is joyously written and provides the reader with a clear and valuable understanding of the stepping stones on the road to enlightenment.

William Meader, Author of SHINE FORTH, The Soul's Magical Destiny
Oregon, USA

Contents

Dedication v
Acknowledgement vii
Foreword ix
Glossary of Terms Used Throughout this Book xv
Author's Note xix
- What this book is about xix
- My first contact with spirit xx
- My work with the Ancestral Group Soul xxv

Chapter 1 - Spiritual Teaching 1
- What is Spirit? 1
- What is the Spirit World? 3
- What is Spiritual Teaching? 5
- What is the Purpose of Life? 8
- How Do I Find My Purpose? 11
- What is the Difference between Spirit, Soul and Personality? 11
- What is the Personality? 15
- What is the Ego? 15
- What is an Aura? 15
- What are guides and teachers? 16
- What is a Master? 17
- Is there a relationship between Master and pupil? If so, how can we tell? 19
- What Influence should they Have on Our Lives? 21

Chapter 2 - The Seven Major Rays of Creation 22
- What is a Ray? 22
- Definition of the Rays 25

Chapter 3 - Stepping Stones – Spiritual & Human 33
- What are these stepping stones? 33
- How do we find them? 34
- How do they help us? 34

Chapter 4 - Soul Lessons 35
- What are these? 35
- How do we understand these? 36

Chapter 5 - Soul Healing, Soul Understanding 38
- What Is meant by this? 38
- What Is Spiritual Healing? 38
- Healing with the Ancestors 40
- What Are Chakras or Centres In the Body? 40
- What Are Spiritual Qualities? 41
- How can Soul Understanding help me to heal myself? 42

Chapter 6 - Group Souls 44
- What is meant by a group soul? 44
- What is Group Soul Recognition? 46
- What is a Soul Mate? 48
- What is a Twin Soul? 48
- What is the Ancestral Group Soul? 49
- Group Ancestral Soul – So Who are they? 54
- How do we do this? 55

Chapter 7 - Spiritual Freedom 62
- What is meant by this? 62
- What is Indoctrination, Conditioning, Perception? 62
- How do we free ourselves? 63
- What is meant by Consciousness? 63
- What is meant by Awareness? 64

- How Do We Know the Difference Between Intuition and Our Imagination?..............64
- How Do We Aspire to A Higher Level?..............66

Chapter 8 - Karma & Past Lives 84
- What is Karma?..............84
- What can we learn from past lives?..............84
- Is Karma a punishment?..............86
- What does it really mean?..............86

Chapter 9 - Deeper Knowledge of the Spiritual Path..............88
- What are Symbols?..............88
- Synchronicity..............91
- What is a Mystic?..............91
- How do we bring mysticism into a living reality?..............92
- What is a practical mystic?..............93
- What are Initiations?..............94
- What are the elements?..............96
- What is Gnosis?..............96

Chapter 10 - Where do we go from here?..............102
- How does the knowledge of the spiritual world help us with the pressures of living?..............102
- How do we walk the Spiritual Path?..............105
- How do we bridge the gap between life on earth and the world of spirit?..............106
- What is there after this life on earth?..............107
- The greatest journey we can ever take..............109

Glossary of Terms Used Throughout this Book

Absolute Being

Also, called the Creator. Some may call this Being God as it is exemplified by orthodoxy. However, when I refer to the Absolute Being in this book, I mean THE Absolute Being. Above creation, above orthodoxy terminology. This can also be described as The Breath, The Force, The Energy that sustains all life. It is worth noting that our planet, Earth, is not a sacred planet, and it is only part of one Universe. There are many Universes, Solar Systems and Constellations of which little is known.

Ages

Our soul lessons take us through the 12 signs of the Zodiac and each sign is described as an Age (e.g. currently on earth we are leaving the Piscean Age and entering the Aquarian Age). Both Ages are very much influencing events around the globe. An Age is approx. 2,400 years

Akashic

These are known as accurate records which are imprinted in the ether as our soul goes through the earthly life's experiences. Each time our soul learns a lesson it is imprinted in the Akashic records. This can never be incorrect – as our soul learns, so it is written.

Antahkarana

This is the bridge between the soul and the spirit. This is the Bridge that connects the lower to the higher (the personality to the soul, and the soul to the spirit)

Astral
This is the level that we often go to in our sleep state. It is related to our emotions and it is the level most often seeing by mediums and clairvoyants. It is also the level that the mass of humanity may find themselves in once they have left the physical body.

Atmic
This is the highest level after the buddhic consciousness. Only those who have attained very high degrees of initiations are aware of this level.

Buddhic
A state of consciousness which is attained once we have gone through the emotional and mental planes. To reach this level we would have found enlightenment.

Devas
These Beings are on a different life stream from the human. More in line with the Angelic and Natural Kingdom. They help humans as do those of the Angelic and Natural Kingdoms.

Etheric
The next level after the physical. We all have an etheric body which is a replica of the physical but without all the restraints, emotions and thoughts of the human body.

Logos
These could be described as Gods who are responsible for different universal systems, i.e. there is a Planetary Logos, a Solar Logos and a Cosmic Logos in our specific Universe.

Monad/monadic
Again, referring to the highest – God or Atmic

Root-races
There are seven root races thus far known to humanity. These are:
The Polarian
The Hyperborean
The Lemurian
The Atlantean

The Aryan (our current root-race)
There will be two others after our current one of which hardly anything is known.

Every root-race has seven sub-races. We are presently in the fifth sub-race of the Fifth Root Race which is the Aryan.

Author's Note

What this book is about

This book is about basic spirituality. It is about answering those initial first questions that come when an individual has awakened to the spiritual path.

I first started writing this book about 20 years ago, and over the years, I have added some bits but in the main it just stayed in the background. I have been facilitating talks and workshops for many years on 'Soul Healing, Soul Understanding' and several people over the years have said 'you should write all this down'. However, my time was taken up with work, counselling, family, friends etc. so very little time to sit down and write. Nevertheless, when I retired from office work last year, I knew that the time was right to continue my writings. I gave myself a couple of years to do this, however, little did I know that spirit was determined that I was not going to have any free time and it was like being thrown at the deep end but in fairness spirit were very patient, understanding and helpful in encouraging me to complete this book. It was made very clear to me that I just had to get on with it.

What I have found over the years is that there are many people who are just becoming aware of the world of spirit. It is like an awakening for them and whilst there are countless books on spirituality on the shelves and indeed many wonderful teachers to learn from, there are not that many on what I would call 'basic spirituality', answering the kind of questions that have been asked of me by many who have come to my talks/workshops.

This book is probably not for those who have a more profound knowledge and experience of spirituality. This book is simply about bringing knowledge of the spiritual world to those who have started asking questions, for example 'Who am I?' 'What is it all about?' I hope to reach those who are awakening, with the desire to allay any fears or concerns people still have about the world of spirit. There truly is nothing to be afraid of. It is only fear based on lack of understanding that is keeping that door closed to us. It is our right to know who we are and what our purpose is. However, because there are so many pitfalls on the path, I would strongly advise you to use discernment and discrimination when you start your search.

So, I would like to start at the beginning, how I learned. Following the path of spirit is a very long process. It truly is like stepping stones. If our aspirations or ideals are too high, then at times we may be disappointed and even disillusioned. But my advice would be – don't give up. Pick yourself up and continue the journey. It is a journey of frustration, puzzlement and confusion but nevertheless it is a journey of wonder! Maybe some prickly thorns along the way but the ultimate goal, reaching that top of the mountain, will make it all worthwhile. I am still stepping on new stones, I am still learning!

My first contact with spirit

My own contact with spirit came in my early years. As a child, I was blessed to have a maternal grandmother who was a healer. She healed with herbs and there were many times when she used her healing knowledge to heal childhood ailments. In my childhood, I was brought up in the Rock of Gibraltar where my family originate from. Although I was born in the UK, I spent my childhood in Gibraltar just after the Second World War. In those days one had to pay for medical treatment and therefore having a grandmother who was a natural healer was a great asset. Mamaja and I would go out for walks regularly to nearby gardens and as a child I could see the nature spirits. It was both a source of wonderment and a joy for me. I was so lucky to have a grandmother who had incredible insight herself and was both supportive and encouraging. She made the world of spirit seem natural. She was also very wise.

As I grew up and my grandmother passed over, I closed the door to my earlier contacts with spirit and simply got on with life. It was only after my mother's passing that I realised 'this is it', I knew my mother wasn't just buried six foot under. I knew there was more and so I allowed that door to open. It opened like floodgates! At first I didn't know what had hit me. I tried to get help from different sources to try and explain how I should deal with this. Although I received some support, no one really gave me the understanding nor the training or guidance I needed to deal with what was given to me. So in the end I had to rely on spirit and my own common sense. I realised that the only true help and support would have to come from within.

When the floodgates opened, I could 'see', I could 'hear' and automatic writing was also used to help me along the way. I was encouraged to search and search and read many books but slowly I was taught and realised that it was through my own meditations and attunement that I would get the help I was seeking. So slowly I allowed spirit back into my life. In one of my most wonderful meditations my mother came and explained what her passing had been like. I need to explain here that at the time of her passing my Mum was in hospital where they were trying to control her very high blood pressure. She died of a heart attack. I remember her words in my meditation so vividly.

My mother's words went like this:

'I opened my eyes and thought I was still in hospital, in the same bed, and then I realised that my husband was standing there next to me, smiling and holding my hand. How can this be, I thought? He has been dead for 23 years. But there he was beaming at me and welcoming me. Then another man came up to the other side of the bed and it was my brother, Victor, who had passed on 15 years before. They gently told me I had died and was now in the world of spirit. I was so upset at this because it was so sudden and I had left my daughter on her own. My son was married and had a family but my daughter lived with me and I had left her. My husband then told me to look at the opposite wall and there I saw a movie screen. In it I saw my

daughter's life moving forward and the incredible spiritual work in the years ahead. My husband helped me to understand that she would not be free to do this if I stayed on earth. Acceptance came over me as I understood. I then looked at one side of the room, and the wall had disappeared and instead I saw beautiful gardens. By the entrance, I saw my own mother smiling and beckoning me forward. Both my husband and my brother helped me get out of bed and I walked to the entrance of the gardens. Then straight in front of me between two trees stood the most beautiful Light Being I had ever seen. To me it was like seeing Jesus. I just walked forward, almost ran straight into his arms. I knew then that I had come home'.

After this meditation, any fears or concern about death completely left me. I was also at peace with my mother's passing and just knew she was OK. In some ways, this released me so I could get on with my life. I trusted totally that spirit had called me to work and this I have done for the last 35 years. As time moves on, I become more and more aware of a world enriched with mystery, awe, joy, abundance of life and, above all, a world that is a continuation of who I am. I know that I will not die. I know that I will one day shake off the physical raiment and continue my journey through other worlds. There is so much I want to know, so much I want to learn. There was a time, a few years ago, when I was so impatient to move on. I have had a heart condition for many years. This is prevalent in both sides of my family and in the main, all my family go young. So far, I have survived both my parents and my brother, umpteen uncles and aunts and two cousins. However, I still have to surpass my grandmother. This wise old lady stayed with us until she was 84. But I have also accepted that there is the right time for my soul. When my work is finished, then I will go. In another meditation, I saw myself as elderly lying on a bed and then a beautiful Being came for me and held out his hand and said it was time to go. I remember saying' 'But my work isn't finished', and he said, 'Others will continue', and so I got out of bed and went with him into the Light.

There is a right time for us all. We all have a purpose, a culmination of our journey on earth and no matter how much we may struggle against life, or whether we believe in the world of spirit or not, when the call comes, our soul will respond and the angel of death will cut that silver cord. Then we will awaken to our true home!

Over many years, since my first contact with spirit, I have been conscious that there were two of me. I worked in the business world for many years and it seems to me that I was manifesting another aspect of myself. The lessons learned however were invaluable and although difficult at times I am grateful for these experiences. It was only after a heart bypass when I had to leave the business world behind and concentrate on my spiritual work, that I really found myself. I found my soul work. It has been a most tremendous journey. This journey has been full of joy, of pain and disillusion but also one of gratitude for the many blessings I have received. After all these years working with spirit, I am still in awe and amazed with the wonder of the spirit world. For over twenty years I worked in the healing work with a spiritual organisation but I retired from this last year. My work today is mostly concentrated on spiritual counselling, talks, workshops and now writing. It is such a truth that the longer I go on in this work, the less I know. The panorama gets wider and wider. Each time I glimpse a truth, I am given yet another stepping stone to move on to.

I would encourage anyone who yearns to be in touch with their spiritual side to set aside time on a regular basis to gradually attune themselves to the spirit world. We have companions of old, messengers of light, guides and angels, waiting to help us. We just need to be open, without fear, to their guidance. What helped me in those early years was to gently use the in and out breath to quieten down the senses. On the in-breath I would think of the words LOVE, LIGHT and on the out breath, I would think AND PEACE. I would do this for about 10 to 15 minutes at first, then I just naturally went into a meditation. These were such valuable times for me as it was then that my spirit companions brought me many images and as I have always been able to visualise, I learned so much from these sessions.

Admittedly, I didn't always quite 'get' at first what they were trying to teach me but slowly over the years I have learned how to interpret the symbols they have given me. These moments with my spiritual companions are ones that I cherish. I have learned to respect their guidance and know it is right for me, even though I may be asking for something completely different. Over the years, I have become aware of my ancestral group soul and little by little, it was made clear to me that this is the work I needed to dedicate my life to. Working with the ancestral group is a joy and wonder and I have been truly amazed how many of my clients have been helped.

Of particular joy for me is to see how my parents, my grandmother and my brother are in the world of spirit. I know that my mother especially is working with children from third world countries who pass over. She is one of many helpers from spirit who greet these children when they pass on and look after them. My father often works with me as a helper and guide. His main work though is in teaching craft to others. My father was always very good with his hands and used to make wonderful models from wood work. He made a small replica of St. Paul's Cathedral, the Santa Maria, one of Columbus' ships, and a little chapel for my mother where she could place the icon of Jesus. His work was so intricate but sadly, he never had enough time on earth to develop this craft (he died very young at 45) but he has done so in spirit and really loves sharing his knowledge with others who wish to develop their own skills. My brother was always involved in charitable works whilst on earth and indeed a leading light in them. His work now takes him to the cultural field where he is pursuing his interest in multi-cultural education. When my grandmother first came back to me from spirit I did not recognise her. She looked so young and vibrant. It was only when she showed me the image of how she had been when I knew her, that I understood. But now when she comes, she comes in her new body of light. Her work in spirit now is to participate in the Halls of Wisdom, learning and teaching. She and I have been together in several lifetimes, particularly in Mayan cultures.

Another great joy for me has been the contact with my Teacher and Master. I have come to trust and respect the way that I have been led. Not always easy, but I do appreciate that I needed some sharp lessons along the path. This contact has remained true and steadfast over the years. I have never been left alone. I have always been aware of a strong and gentle presence supporting me. This presence has been my rock. He has come in different guises over the years and has at times guided me over to another Teacher who has been instrumental in helping me over a specific work. No names are necessary although I know who he is. In this book, I give him full acknowledgement as without his guidance and teaching, I would not have been able to do my work. Above all though, I am so grateful for his wisdom and his unconditional love. Not to mention his wonderful sense of humour and never-ending patience.

My work with the Ancestral Group Soul

In my counselling work with the Ancestors, I always call upon them before a client comes so that they can in turn call upon the Ancestors of the client to bring them whatever support or guidance they may need. With the Ancestors' help, I am given insights to a client's past lives where there is usually a thread, a link from those lives to the present one. Even after so many years of doing this work, I am still astonished at how links with past lives can affect a soul in this lifetime. What needs to be remembered is that it is the soul that retains the memory of either emotional or mental experiences. If these experiences have been painful; if a soul has gone through great suffering, the memory of that is retained at soul level and the individual soul can choose when it needs to go back and confront that experience in order to face it and let it go.

Another side to this is that an aspect of an individual's group soul may need help to heal something from the past. Because we are at one with our group soul, the soul on earth has agreed to help another aspect at a deep soul level though not at a conscious level necessarily. In my experience, I have seen how a soul currently on earth may have had an experience of deep hurt that resonates with an aspect of his/her group soul. If the soul on earth is able to go back and understand what happened when and why, then by accepting and acknowledging what happened in a previous life, healing can start to take place. As above, so below. As below, so above.

Those in spirit are always delighted to come forth and help us on earth. They are not up there somewhere floating around in white sheets, just waiting to spook us. They are very real and they are here, right beside us. Our ancestors can bring us so much valuable knowledge about ourselves. Every life is linked.

This work started slowly for me and then it was like a train hurtling me forward. With each stepping stone I understand a little more. I become more and more aware of how our lives are held and guided by something far greater than the little me. I am conscious of my greater Self and have learned over the years how to trust my intuition. This has been my saving grace over the years throughout many difficult situations. I have always known and been able to 'see' through things and, at times, through people. One thing that I have learned from spirit is that there is no hiding place. Truth is truth, however unpalatable it may be. Voicing our truth, when it may not easily be received by others, is not always palatable but one has to learn tact, sensitivity and have the strength and courage to speak and act when it feels absolutely right.

Chapter 1
Spiritual Teaching

What is Spirit?

This is a subject that is both mystifying and disconcerting at the same time. We are all spirit. There has never been a time when we were not spirit. The spirit world is the natural world of creation. The spirit world is a world of Light, a sphere, a plane of consciousness that is our natural home – another level of existence. We were all created as a seed by the Absolute Being, to develop and unfold those spiritual qualities inherent in each one of us. This is a very simplistic way of putting it and for those who wish to study more, there is a wealth of books and teachers available to take you further on the path.

There are as many aspects of creation as there are different levels within each one of us. Here we are referring to the cosmos, made up of multiple universes, solar and planetary systems. With our finite mind, it is impossible to try to figure out the infinite mind. We cannot go there, but we do have a semblance of knowledge, again inherent in us, that gives us some understanding, although infinitesimal. As far as we can ascertain, through the many books of old, the Absolute Being, breathed out an energy, a fire, and life eventually (after aeons and aeons of time) became form. These forms were the initial constellations, planets, cosmic life, solar life and planetary life that we often hear or read about. This is a vast subject needing in-depth study. For those who would like to go further, there are many wonderful books about this.

There are three words which have been given in a number of teachings and which perhaps exemplifies Creation, and these are:

EXPERIMENT – EXPERIENCE – EXPRESSION

The whole of creation is an experiment - an experience that can only be measured by the myriad of forms' expressions.

Above the earth experience, is the etheric and astral, then the mental planes, then the buddhic, then higher levels which are known as atmic levels and even beyond. Each plane has seven levels of experience. Every individual soul will need to develop and unfold to reach the highest degree of realization in order to attain full consciousness and then move onto other planes of existence within the cosmos.

In my search for spirit, and initially coming from an orthodox religious upbringing, I thought that God was the ultimate. Little by little I started to think of the Creator of all life. Lately, I have concluded that if we truly believe that there is no beginning and no end, how can there be a Creator. A Creator suggests a beginning of something. So now through my own inner search I have realised that there is an Architect of all life, the Absolute Being – an Intelligence well beyond our finite minds understanding. Neither He nor She, just It! I believe the Absolute Being to be an immeasurable Energy, a Force which is both creative and destructive – destructive in order to create. Other than this, I can offer no other explanation. So much of what we understand or think we know about Creation is probably mere supposition. Many books have been written by distinguished and learned authors. The Masters themselves have chosen disciples through whom much knowledge has been imparted. It might be worthwhile to remember that we can only be given what we can understand at our level of development. Remember that the Masters too are developing and moving forward. They can see with a wider vision and clarity than we can and are there to help us, to guide us forward along the path. We need also to understand that there is a hierarchy of Masters, of Higher Beings (sometimes also called Monads) who are guiding the whole experience of humanity. Everything that happens has a purpose and a reason, be that of evolution, creation or 'destruction'.

With our finite minds, we can only glimpse at something so huge, so awesome, that is impossible to fathom. Nevertheless, what we do have is that inner knowing that there is something far greater than ourselves, something that we need to reach out and aspire to. Slowly our spirit guides us forward along a very long and often arduous journey. This journey is part of the evolution of life. All life is evolving constantly. Nothing stands still. This includes the planetary system, the universes and the Logos. Life is perpetual motion.

The earth planet is only a small fraction of what there exists in this incredible universe. And there are other universes, other galaxies, other cosmic spheres.

It is truly a wondrous journey!

What is the Spirit World?

The spirit world is our true home. This may appear rather basic and simplistic but nevertheless a true fact. A home where there are many companions and loved ones awaiting us. In the spirit world there are many levels or spheres of consciousness and we will go to whichever one our soul has reached in its path of evolution. We would be limiting ourselves if we think of loved ones as solely those we have known or loved in this earthly life. There are companions of our soul who have been with us in other lives and have shared our lessons. There are those who are karmically linked to us until we have cleared that karma. We all belong to group souls and aspects of that group soul incarnates at differing times according to the condition of what needs to be learned appertaining to the group soul. Whatever we learn, whatever we achieve, is also realised by our group soul. All experiences are recorded at group soul level and in the Akashic records. As we learn, they learn. As they learn (in other circumstances and experiences), we learn. And importantly, we grow.

Our home, our level of consciousness, in spirit will be determined by our endeavours on earth, in this lifetime and in previous ones. There is perfect justice, perfect outworking of spiritual law. Natural spiritual law is just and perfect. There is good order and no one escapes this. In spirit we cannot cheat, lie or deceive by thought, word or action. What we are, and what we have attained, is imprinted on the ether for all to see. What or rather who we are deep inside will show like a fingerprint, it is individual to us, it cannot lie nor can we cover it up. There is no escaping in spirit.

But in these realms everyone is constantly learning and therefore understanding and compassionate and above all non-judgmental. There are many teachers, helpers who come to support us and help us to understand our lives on earth and the lessons we gained by those experiences. They will help us face our weaknesses and our qualities. With their guidance we will then be able to judge ourselves, or rather assess our past endeavours, and plan our next stage of development.

The spirit world is vibrant with life, there is plenty of activity and there is also a sense of peace which underlies all activity. This is the peace of belonging, a knowing that although all at first may seem amazing and possibly confusing, we have survived death; that life does go on in other spheres. There is much to learn and the wonder is that there is no time limit in which to learn.

The spirit world is also fun. It is not all the serious stuff of learning and getting things right or floating in a nebulous form. Our friends in spirit have a tremendous sense of humour and it can be wonderful to establish a rapport with companions who we may think at first are unknown to us but in reality, are well known to us. You will meet many kindred spirits who have gone through similar experiences as yourself and will be able to understand and share their experiences with you. There will be many reunions with old friends and loved ones – a time of sharing and joy. There is music, there is dancing, there is healing, there is learning. There is also the opportunity to continue giving in service. The material and physical problems of the earthly life will no longer trouble you. You will gain a greater understanding of earthly conditions and happenings.

There will be opportunities when you are ready to help in the healing and care of others if this is your wish. This could be in the healing temples or hospitals to help those souls who have gone through great physical duress during their time on earth and are now in need of care and healing. This healing is of course for the soul as the memory of the physical suffering is stressed on the soul of the individual. Working with children may be more your line and if this is so there are a number of ways in which this can be done. There are those children who have starved to death from different countries or who through malnutrition have suffered great physical diseases, they will need very tender and gentle care. My own mother works with these children and is there to welcome them as they enter the spirit world. There are children who have been very cruelly treated on earth whose souls need a great deal of gentle loving, nurturing and reassurance. Perhaps you may prefer to work with older children whose physical parents are still on earth and need a spirit mother or father.

My contacts with spirit are so natural. Perhaps this is one of the reasons why I quite enjoy being on my own. Truly I am not alone – none of us are. I am helped by my awareness of the spirit world. My companions and my work with the ancestral group soul are a source of wonder and joy. Sometimes I am perplexed when I don't quite get what they are trying to teach me, but they are unfailingly patient.

The above is truly very simplistic. It is a starting ground. As we unfold and develop our true spiritual nature there are other spheres, other planets with whom we have an association, and we may choose to move on to these to continue our search. There is constant motion, nothing stops still. Energy evolves. It is like the waves on the seashore. It comes in and ebbs out, similar to the in and out breath. This is life. This is the force, the energy that moves us and holds all life, all kingdoms of nature, in its sphere. Light and Darkness – all One!

What is Spiritual Teaching?

What is meant by spiritual teaching? Very simply, it is guidance given by those in the world of spirit to provide us with a better understanding of the big questions of life, such as:

- What is the purpose of life?
- What is there after this life on earth?

- What is the spirit world?
- How do we bridge the gap between life on earth and life in the spirit world?
- How to recognise who we truly are?
- How do we free ourselves from indoctrination?

…..and many more.

The general concept of the spirit world is of wandering ghosts who come back to spook us or to give us messages through a medium, be this by direct contact or by other phenomena like ouji board or séances etc.

In reality, many of these are not true contacts as these phenomena are related usually to the astral plane which is illusory and therefore only pertinent to the plane of emotions. That these emotions are very real to the majority of people is an accepted fact but the fundamental aspect of spiritual teaching is to bring enlightenment to each soul so as to disperse the illusory concepts surrounding humanity, thereby lifting the veil between the earthly plane and the 'true and real' spiritual world.

To most people the spirit world, if they ever think of it, is something that one finds out about after death. Indeed, many don't even acknowledge a spirit world and believe that this (the earthly planet) is all there is. Even so, to those who half-believe in a spirit world the idea that one should start preparing now for an after-life is somewhat incredulous. Yet, this is the most tremendous journey that we will ever take. So, the general perception of a spirit-life is rather vague and one that most people prefer not to think about let alone discuss or read about. However, there are those who have the 'gift' of contact with the spirit world whose pure motives help others to cope with grief and bereavement.

Hurdles and Obstacles along the way

The next major hurdle when approaching the topic of spiritual life is *fear*. Fear in the minds of the people who know nothing about the world of spirit and who have concocted in their minds impressions of something possibly a little spooky, evil and unwholesome. As fear is based on lack of understanding, then the obvious step here is to educate ourselves to remove this fear. But this is not so easy as one finds oneself battling with the kind of fear that has been a conditioned factor in the minds of people for possibly centuries and indeed has been played upon by orthodox religions to keep the people within their control.

Then of course there is *prejudice*. Someone may have heard a story about someone else who had a frightening experience with the world of spirit, or such like, which is all rather vague and therefore the assumption that the world of spirit is not to be messed about with is arrived at. Some may have had contacts with mediums where messages may have been a little dubious or hard to accept so the warning has gone out to avoid contacts with spirit. There are also many fraudsters disguised as mediums who have created a very different unreal world to the unknowing and concretised their beliefs and fears of the spirit world.

To some, who may frequent mediums, there is the belief that the spirit world only consists of the astral levels and that their loved ones who have departed should be there to assist them in every possible way. They are then disillusioned when this does not happen.

So, in effect, there are many prejudices and fears to overcome in the guidance and teaching of the world of spirit. The spiritual life is simple to live once we have broken through barriers of prejudice, illusion and fear. This statement may appear naïve in its simplicity, but, if a person is really interested in learning how to live a truly spiritual life, and is willing to search further, then as the path unfolds and as knowledge is gained, they realise the true meaning of this statement.

One of the first things to accept is that we are never alone. Around us are helpers from spirit including our very own particular guide who has been with us since birth and has pointed the way for us by the lessons and circumstances we have been placed in. Our helpers vary from time to time according to the particular lesson we need to learn. Let us now take the first point previously mentioned.

What is the Purpose of Life?

This is really two-fold. On the one hand, there is creation and evolution and on the other there is the purpose and unfoldment of spiritual qualities of the individual person.

If we assume that the Absolute Being no doubt had a purpose in conceiving creation as we know it, then perhaps the purpose of creation and the evolution of humanity in general is a concept which the average person can only dimly be aware of and in fact is such a deep and vast subject that the average mind boggles at even the thought of it. It is virtually impossible for the average thinker to imagine the thinking of the Absolute Being or even visualise the purpose of creation itself, let alone get to grips with the evolution of humanity, the universes, solar systems, planetary systems, the cosmos, the galaxies, the different great Ages and the root-races and the different kingdoms of nature. The idea that other universes exist outside our own planetary system may seem incredulous and too awesome and vast a subject to penetrate any further, certainly in this book. But the purpose of spiritual teaching is to bring enlightenment on even this vast and often misconstrued and misunderstood subject.

Let's concentrate on the purpose of life for an individual

Every individual is born with a specific soul purpose and it is the soul, which is the vehicle, the consciousness, for the spirit, that guides the person through the lessons that the individual needs to learn in any particular lifetime. Before it comes back to incarnation, each soul carries with it the knowledge of its journey through the Akashic records and, with this insight, chooses its own parents and the environment and country which it needs in order to develop or strengthen a quality or overcome and control a specific weakness (which is only an un-developed quality). Everyone is always in the right place at the right time, no matter what the circumstances, to enable the soul to learn from that particular situation or circumstance.

We engender the environment and the circumstances which will help us to unfold those qualities. It will really help us if we can recognise and accept that we have two sides – the outer personality, which is called the character, the side which the outside world normally sees, and the inner 'us' (the soul) which is in fact guiding us from the inner planes and which can, if allowed, help us to face our challenges and trials with calm and tranquillity knowing that all these trials are part of the process of evolution and initiation.

So the first point is to try and differentiate between the outer and the inner you. This can be done by going on a journey of self-discovery. To go on this journey one needs to be very honest with oneself and be prepared to face realities and truths that may prove hard to take for the outer personality, at first, but which will slowly and steadily release and give strength to the inner soul.

When a soul incarnates it comes with a dual function or purpose. First, to develop and expand its own inner qualities and, secondly, to work with its group soul towards the evolution of humanity. These are both inter-related because as you progress and learn yourself you are lifting and expanding the consciousness of humanity in general. This naturally applies greatly to our own surroundings and our relationships with other people.

The soul needs the daily contact with people to learn its lessons. What may seem to you to be struggles, anxieties and conflicts are in fact to be embraced as they are the very means by which we evolve. Life is all about learning, evolving and expanding. It is a fact, by natural law, that we are constantly changing and learning. Even our sufferings, as real and painful as they are, provide our soul with tremendous opportunities to increase spiritual knowledge. Whatever comes to us is either a lesson to expand our knowledge and develop our qualities and/or an opportunity to repay a debt which we may have inflicted on another person in this life or a previous one.

If we could accept that in life we attract the 'good' or the 'bad' by our own attitude and endeavours and that nothing happens by chance or misfortune, then perhaps acceptance of life may be easier. Whatever comes to us is something that we have attracted to ourselves by the way we think, speak or act, whether in this present life or in a previous one.

Every single individual has a purpose. Everyone is important in the plan of the Absolute Being for the evolution of creation. We are all cells in the body of the Logos We are all seeds planted by the Creator and for this seed to grow and blossom into a beautiful flower, we need the nourishment of our endeavours and our efforts. This nourishment is given by our capacity to learn and grow in this training ground of earth. We choose our own training ground and the quality we would like to develop within a particular incarnation. We choose our own environment, families, nation and race to provide us with the best equipment with which to learn our lessons. However, it is worth remembering that this choosing, however odd it may seem, is done purely at soul level. Before incarnation, we will look back at our Akashic records with our guide, our inner teacher, and analyse our experiences and summarise what lessons still have to be learned.

There are times of course when a soul comes back to earth to serve and to teach. Sometimes also a soul may decide to take advantage of the 'credits' it has stored up in previous lives and enjoy an easier life. Karma plays a part here but more on this later.

One of the most important aspects of the purpose of incarnation is to learn how to live and work with others. By giving loving service, wherever we are, we develop the heart centre which is the seat, the very centre of our being. Through love, we can accomplish our purpose for it is only by giving in true service that we lose ourselves, we lose the outer 'I', the personality and in loving ourselves we find the spirit within, the real inner us, the self, the breath of all life, our own divinity, the I AM. This is what is known as at-one-ment with the Absolute Being, this is the unity of all creation. We need to recognise that the outer self, the personality that we are known by, is not our real Self; the personality is the outer garment, the coat that we have put on for this incarnation and this outer garment has been fashioned by the experiences we have brought over from a previous life and also by the environment we have been brought up in. Our prejudice, our likes and dislikes, our fears, all these are the results of past experiences, present conditioning, national and racial habits.

Our purpose is to recognise who we are and what we need to do to and to develop our spiritual qualities. This can only be done by living life in the outer world and by giving service to life.

How Do I Find My Purpose?

By observing your life, present and past, what were, and what are, the things that you really enjoy and enjoyed doing? What are the things that people say you are good at? Your purpose may be at a very deep soul level, but there are likely to be signs in your outer life which provide vital clues. Go into your own journey of self-discovery. It can be both exciting and scary but extremely worthwhile when you discover your own jewel. This is a journey which will reveal who you truly are - not just the outer personality, although that does have a significance, but who you truly are at a soul level. Reach for those jewels deep within yourself. Here's a little exercise to get to know yourself better.

Getting to know yourself – an exercise to help

Write down on one side of the page those qualities that you think you have. On the other side of the page write down those qualities that other people say about you. Compare! How well do you know yourself? Equally, write down the not so positive things about yourself; what do others say? You may have true friends or family who will be only too happy to help you out with this one! Compare! Does it make interesting reading? So, is it now time to start working on yourself. Observe yourself in daily life. Observe your reactions. Be your own Silent Watcher. Remember, there is no criticism here, no beating yourself up because you may be aware of something about yourself which you don't like. The beauty of this exercise is that it is giving you knowledge – self-knowledge. Be totally honest. No one but you need know about this. What a wondrous opportunity to free yourself. Don't be afraid to take that step forward.

What is the Difference between Spirit, Soul and Personality?

Let us understand first that there are three parts of us, the outer self (the PERSONALITY), the higher self (SOUL) and the monad (the SPIRIT).

The **Personality** is the part of our self which we call our character. This consists of our Emotions, Thoughts and Physical body. The Personality is swayed by our emotions, by our thoughts, by our environment, by our conditioning, by our mental perception of life. It is the side that we show to people. For many, it is the only aspect that they are aware of.

The **Soul** is our conscience, that part of us which knows our path, knows what lessons we need in order to evolve and unfold. The part that we so often ignore because we are not listening, the part which fear keeps imprisoned. Our soul guides us even though we may not be aware of the difference between the Soul and the Personality.

The **Spirit** is the direct line from the Absolute. It uses the Soul as its vehicle to guide our path. It is the Silent Watcher. It is in at-one-ment with all creation. It is our very essence, our breath, the energy that sustains us. Spirit is the life-impulse.

The Personality is the vehicle for the Soul and the Soul is the vehicle for the Spirit.

First of all, let us define Spirit

As has been said above, we are all spirit and there has never been a time when we were not spirit for the simple reason that spirit is the pure essence of our being. From the moment that our seed was breathed forth from the Absolute Being, we are spirit, pure spirit. However, spirit has no form, it is pure energy. It was the original experiment. The initial impulse – the force. Therefore, to know Itself it needed to experience Itself through matter but matter is too dense and matter would be destroyed by the pure energy, the pure fire, the force of spirit. Thus, the soul became the vehicle for the spirit. The soul is a consciousness. It senses, it feels, it remembers, but it has no form. Hence, the soul needed a vehicle, a form, in which to express itself, in which to manifest. So, this is where the personality, the form, the outer body we are familiar with came into being.

As a reminder and putting it simply, the body is the vehicle for the soul as the soul is the vehicle for the spirit.

More on the Soul

Throughout history we have been told by many spiritual teachers and prophets that life is eternal, so therefore one is led to assume that there must be something more than the physical body which continues after our experiences on earth. It seems also to suggest that whilst we may discard the personality/the material form, something else continues. This something may be called many things by different teachers, philosophers and prophets. I am comfortable in calling this the spirit, the soul consciousness. Whatever we call it, if we believe that there is more to us than the physical form, then something else must continue.

So what is this soul consciousness? We hear people speak of spirit, or soul. As I see it, the spirit is the very essence of our being. It is the prime motivator. It is the breath, the energy, the force. Spirit has no form because it is not an entity. It is what makes life *be*. It is the *I Am*. There is nothing in the universe that is not motivated by spirit, by energy. It is the pure essence. However, because it is an essence, a breath, an energy, it needs to experience and express Itself and It uses the vehicle of the soul for this experiment. Whether we can accept or believe this or not, does come down to our own belief system and our own experiences.

Nevertheless, let us just for this moment hold this thought and let us accept for now that there is a soul, that there is a spirit and allow ourselves to believe that we are far more than the outer shell, more than the personality that we portray to the world. First, let us accept that we are spirit, that there never has been a time when we were not spirit. But spirit is an essence, it has no form it is pure essence. It is like the Alpha and the Omega. In its purest essence, it is the *I Am*. So it needs a vehicle through which to experience Itself, thus we have the soul.

It is worth repeating - the soul is a consciousness. It has the pure essence of spirit within Itself but it needs to experience what It is. It has the facility for gaining knowledge. It has a memory. It is this consciousness, this memory that moves from one life to another, retaining the experiences learned at each level. However, the soul has no form. So therefore it needs a form. This is where our physical bodies come in. The body, the personality, is the vehicle for the soul as the soul is the vehicle for the spirit. It is through life's many experiences that the soul can unfold and develop its spiritual qualities; it accumulates all its knowledge and experience so that one day we shall arrive at that final spot of the Alpha and the Omega where we can truly say *I Know that I Am*. As we do this, we can attain that confidence and serenity in the knowledge that our spirit, through the vehicle of the soul consciousness, will continue.

This means that we truly have as much time as we need to know ourselves, time to assimilate the experiences that we face each lifetime. Every experience, whether good or bad, has a purpose – a lesson learned at a deeper level of understanding. But are these lessons, these experiences, purely personal or are we something far greater than we give ourselves credit for? The knowledge that we could be more than the outer personality is both exciting and scary. So what are we?

The soul itself has a three-fold nature; it is self-conscious (personality), it is group conscious (soul) and it is (at a very deep level) God-conscious (spirit). The soul has no personal nor individual ambitions or individual interests. It really is not at all interested in the ambitions, intentions or intricacies of its personality. The soul exists as a consciousness and it is there to guide the personality through its multiple experiences. The purpose of life is about the personality, the individual person realising that there is more to life than just the physical. Slowly, following many lifetimes, the soul guides the personality to reach a stage when it becomes aware there is something greater than the physical. The personality becomes aware of itself as the soul, with soul powers, soul relationships and soul purpose. When the personality realises this, it begins to lift its awareness to acknowledging, perhaps initially in a small measure, that it is part of a group soul.

If we accept the existence of a soul, of a spirit, then perhaps the next question is – how does this work? What have I been before? Where have I been before? What have I learned? What shall I be in the future? If we have all been before, then there is obviously more than the little 'me' of the present earthly body around. Am I part of something bigger? Nowadays on earth, we are able to look up records and find our current life ancestry which can be delightful and very interesting. But if we have an earthly ancestry, it seems reasonable to suppose that we also have a spiritual ancestral tree. If so, who are these ancestors and what part do they play in our lives? What records can we look up? What exactly is our spiritual DNA? (see Chapter on the Ancestral Group Soul).

What is the Personality?

The personality is our outer character in this lifetime. Our personality is our likes and dislikes, our emotions, our thoughts. It is the image we portray to others in everyday life. Before our awakening our personality is ruled by our emotions and our thoughts, but slowly as awakening comes, the awareness that there is something greater than the outer self begins to assert itself. Gradually our soul begins to make its presence felt and we no longer react from our emotions or thoughts. Our personality is very necessary for our growth. It is by going through every challenge, every experience, that we develop and unfold. Our personality, encompassing both the emotional and mental bodies, has to find a point of balance between them. Only then can we truly allow the spirit within to guide our lives. We need to bring spirituality down into matter so that matter is transmuted by the light within.

What is the Ego?

In some writings, the ego is often described as the higher Self, a Higher Expression also known as the Monad. However, ego is often the term used to describe the personality, the outer shell, the character that we show to the outside world. Could also be described as the arrogant part of yourself. In this book when I refer to ego, I am speaking of the outer personality, not the higher Self.

What is an Aura?

An aura is a field of energy which emanates from the physical body and encircles it. As each chakra/centre of our bodies unfold in spiritual qualities and development, the colour which appertains to each particular chakra grows in intensity. Depending on our unfoldment, these colours will reverberate around us and our auras may change according to how we are learning and developing along the spiritual path. For example, if an individual is a very calm and tranquil soul, who has balanced emotions and the mind, then very possibly the colour BLUE would be very distinct and strong in his aura. If an individual has developed his higher consciousness and has great understanding of the spiritual path, then the colour GOLD would be most prominent, especially around the crown chakra. Auras are an indication of how we have progressed along the spiritual path and the qualities we have unfolded. More than one colour may surround us at any time, depending upon our perception, unfoldment and moods. More on colours in a later chapter.

What are guides and teachers?

Each one of us has guides and helpers. These guides may be companions of old, past ancestors or those who have chosen to serve through helping an earthling to unfold their spiritual path. Often our guides are from our group soul (*more on group souls in another chapter*) and they are with us to ensure that we go through those soul lessons which we agreed to prior to our birth on earth. Spiritual law is very clear in that our guides cannot, and will not, interfere with our choices – they are there merely to give us support and encouragement to go through our experiences, however painful or difficult they may be. Even though often in life we may feel we are alone and abandoned, we must try never to forget that there is a group of souls who truly hold out their arms in loving support, who pick us up each time we fall. Our lessons, our challenges, are our soul choices. We make these choices before we come into incarnation because at that level we know, we understand, what we need to learn to further our progress on the spiritual path.

However, it is necessary to say here that each one of us has an inner teacher. This is also known as our Higher Self or sometimes as our Guardian Angel. Our inner teacher knows much better than anyone what we as individual souls need and ensures that the right circumstances for our growth and development come to us.

There are of course other spiritual teachers. We may come across them on our spiritual path and there is an old saying *'by their fruits ye shall know them'*. It is important that we discern the quality of many of these so-called teachers. Teachers can only teach at their own level of understanding and it may be that there comes a point when the student becomes the teacher and needs to move on.

However, there is one vital truth to remember in your search and that is that your best teacher is your own inner heart. It is in your heart and the Light of understanding within where you will discern the voice of truth – has something you have heard ring true for you? If not, then just let it go and move on.

What is a Master?

A Master is an evolved Being who has transcended the Path and through experiences over many lives has reached the stage of evolution where he has mastered the elements of the first four Kingdoms, i.e. the mineral, the vegetable, the animal and the human kingdom He has reached that level of initiation where his Monad (his spirit) has gained control over his personality. He has attained at-one-ment with the Divine Source and his only desire is to serve.

At this level, all Masters are One. They have attuned their bodies to such a degree that all respond to the one chord. Depending on their Monadic Ray, *(more on the rays in later chapters)* the Master will choose to serve a specific cause, one whereby his experiences will be put to the best use in the service of humanity.

There are many Masters of a high degree and a number of others on a lesser degree. That is to say, the Masters of a high degree have reached a higher level of initiation than the other Masters. Usually the Masters of a higher degree do not involve themselves with pupils. Their function is world government and the universal growth and evolution of humanity and of the races. They are involved in different aspects of this development, each having their own department to run. It is like a form of government and they are the Head Ministers with various offices under them to follow and carry out their instructions. They have main disciples who are under their training for a specific task involved in group work or for an individual task that will affect many others.

The Masters of a lesser degree are responsible for the training of pupils and oversee the work in which they are involved with.

Because the Masters have mastered the four lower kingdoms and the natural elements, they are able to come and go in their etheric body as they please depending on the task in hand. Only those in close liaison with them have direct contact or indeed know who they are.

Under the Master's training and tuition there will be a number of disciples and pupils who will receive the tuition necessary according to their stage of evolution. All work with the Master is usually done at soul level and not on the physical level. However, a disciple of a high degree may be consciously aware of his work and his contact with the Master. The Masters do not waste time with those who are not ready. The mass of humanity is in the hands of their own personal guide and higher Self. The Masters are only concerned with those who have reached a certain stage in their evolution and are co-operating with them to further the education and development of mankind.

The Master functions in unison and in accord with the other Masters of the Hierarchy, responding to the needs required to the fulfilment of the Divine Plan. The Master's vision exceeds far beyond the earth and his purpose is to bring the Divine or Spiritual Laws of creation to realisation within the framework of his particular department. The Masters of course work closely with the Lords of Karma. They have control over the elements of nature and can function at any level required according to the needs of his work. He can work on different levels at the same time and will instinctively know when he is needed and will respond corresponding to that need.

Is there a relationship between Master and pupil? If so, how can we tell?

There is a bond between the pupil on the path and the Master on whose Ray he is working. One should recognise that it does not always follow that the pupil will be working with the Master of his Monadic Ray. He may come under the tutelage of the Master of his own soul Ray and yet again, depending on the specific line of service that the pupil may be engaged upon, also come under another Master.

First, to clarify a point and that is that a Master does not make himself or herself known to a pupil until that pupil is ready, that is to say, that the pupil would have reached a stage in his evolution when he will recognise the Master and the work he is involved in. So, that is the first point to bear in mind. The second is that the pupil must learn to distinguish the difference between a Master and other helpers or guides who are with him. A Master will make his presence known to either give certain instructions or to give support or reassurance when the pupil is undergoing a certain heavy or difficult task and needs the stronger force or vibration of the Master.

At this level, the pupil will probably be a disciple in the Master's Ashram. It is usually in the sleep state that the disciple goes to the Ashram to unite with their co-workers and wait to discuss the work in hand or to receive more instructions from the Master. Let me make clear that this relationship between Master and pupil, and pupil with other pupils is one of a strong bond of love and purpose. All of them are united in strength to carry out the work which they have willingly undertaken. Each pupil is personally well known to the Master and if they have been working together for a long time on the same Ray, a very deep love and understanding has developed.

In the Master's care all will be well arranged and over a long period of time great faith and trust is developed. This faith is not of a blind nature but one which has grown from a deep knowledge and understanding of the Master and the work that has been done over many lifetimes. It is also a faith and trust that has developed out of love and respect. A disciple on the path will also go to the Master's Ashram for further teachings on the Ancient Wisdom in order to gain more knowledge on the essence of Universal Life. In the Ashrams pupils meet, at times without necessarily the presence of their Master, to go over and discuss any problems involved in the work, to benefit from each other's knowledge, the sharing of difficulties encountered and to receive support and love from each other. I emphasise that this is all usually at soul level and in your sleep state.

Work in the Ashrams

An Ashram is a training group of advanced disciples who have come together to perform a certain function or task allotted by the Master. Those in this group are joined by their Rays and the development of qualities necessary for the work in hand. A disciple may be in the same Ashram for many lives on earth using these qualities and at the same time playing his or her part in fulfilling the Divine Plan.

A disciple will enter an Ashram when he has reached a stage of evolution where more personal tuition and guidance is needed, which require closer contact with the Master and also when the qualities he has developed can be put to useful service for the whole of humanity. It needs to be remembered that the Ashram the disciple enters will depend on the Ray he is working on and the type of service he is able to give.

An Ashram consists of an inner and outer group. There are Elders who are more attuned to the Master's plan and purpose and it is their task to help the younger members of the Ashrams with guidance, advice and teachings when the Master is engaged in other tasks. To be in the inner group, you do not necessarily have to be out of a physical body. A disciple has reached a stage of evolution where he can function in his higher body whilst still in incarnation.

The unifying quality sustaining each group is love and the purpose to fulfil. There is love for each other, for their Master and the Universal Love that guides their purpose. But this love is not an emotional love, this love is the very essence that binds each together in purpose, brotherhood and service. This love is the factor which embraces the understanding, the courage and strength, the fearlessness to do the work.

What Influence should they Have on Our Lives?

We all reach a stage in our growth, in our development, when we need spiritual understanding, spiritual knowledge. This is when we start searching. At first, we don't always know or understand what we are searching for. However, this is where we trust our inner teacher. Our inner teacher will know whether the motives behind our search are true or whether they are born from a love of glamour and phenomena. This is when synchronicity or symbols may come to us. Maybe we have a question or we are seeking some kind of guidance. Spirit will not always reply direct. But it could be that someone may mention a book or perhaps someone is giving a talk. You may at first not respond but if this happens repeatedly then we would do well to take heed as spirit is very likely trying to communicate a message.

When the time is right and the call goes out from your inner heart, the teacher will come. The awakening may come in different ways, but nevertheless it has come. Listen, read and digest all that you learn. Some of it you may find confusing and beyond your understanding. This is OK, do not feel dejected. We understand things at different levels as we progress on the path. Sometimes we may feel so convinced that we are on the right path only to find out later that it's no longer right for us. This is OK too. It is all about learning, moving forward, digesting, discerning, falling and picking ourselves up every time.

A true teacher will never try to deceive or be so full of their knowledge or exploits along the astral plane. When someone continually just talks about what they can see, or hear then this is their Ego talking. So this is where the wonderful spiritual quality of discernment comes in. Use it wisely!

Chapter 2

The Seven Major Rays of Creation

What is a Ray?

There are Seven Major Rays of Creation. There are also minor ones. Each is distinct and yet inter-related with the others. This is a very deep subject and one which when grasped is extremely helpful in the understanding of both ourselves and our fellow beings For example, if we follow and understood astrology, we could when speaking of a friend or loved one, make a general comment that being an Aquarian makes them very detached, or being an Aries makes them very impulsive or being a Virgo makes them very organised, and so forth. In a sense, the Rays are similar. If we can understand what the Seven Rays mean and how to understand them and how it affects us, or people around us, it can help us understand our lives better.

So what is a Ray? A Ray is an energy, a force, that was breathed from the Absolute Being. It is the energy that has sustained the universal cosmic life. It is the driving force behind what makes us tick. There are many books that have been written on the Seven Rays by past teachers and current sensitives, so there really is a lot of information out there. Understanding the Rays helps us to understand ourselves and those around us. Because when we have that knowledge we can be more tolerant of those around us. We don't use it, for example, as an excuse because someone has behaved in a bad way. We can't justify an act simply by saying, 'Oh well he can't help that because he's third

Ray Leo'. Knowledge of the Rays gives us an understanding about the character of the individual to help us be less judgmental or intolerant.

Understanding the Seven Rays is a vast subject – where did it start, where did it come from, what does it mean in this day and age? There's so many things that are related to the topic of the Seven Rays.

The Seven Rays affect everything about who we are. There is a resonance with the chakras, the centres in the body; there is a resonance with colour; there is a resonance with the different planets. Every Ray represents an aspect of the Divine, emerging from Unity into creation where it is expressed. Each has a subjective aspect as well as an objective one. Each is a stable pure Essence which cannot be changed, but in the human realm the *expression* of each can be perverted through the mis-use of our freewill. However, to the degree that we unfold our innate perfection, the expression flows harmoniously unhindered. Unless man intervenes in a negative way, in the natural realm there is a perfect sevenfold expression of the Rays

Each Ray is governed by a Master also called a Lord or Chohan, and each of us works under the loving care of that particular Lord. We attune to a particular Master according to our level of development and the type of outer or inner work undertaken.

We can through one life come under the influence of a number of Masters again depending on how we respond to the promptings of the inner guiding light and what specific work we have to do. But in general, we respond to the Ray of one Master. All the Rays have an influence in our lives and some may be more predominant than others at any particular stage.

The soul can work on one particular Ray for a very long time but this is not altogether exclusive as it will also function and experience other Rays. Eventually of course all the experiences will blend into one. This is the Christ Light, the White Light that is often spoken about.

We are composed of seven subtle bodies, the physical, etheric, lower astral, astral, mental, buddhic, atmic and each respond to a different Ray. Our personality, the outer us, has a specific Ray, as does the emotional body and the mental body. Most importantly of all the soul also has its own specific Ray. In each lifetime, we portray characteristics of that Ray, whichever one it is. So perhaps the question in your mind right now is, 'Well, how do I know which is the Ray of my emotions, my mind, my soul, my personality.' It's a vast area, but this is where intuition comes in, how well do you know yourself? When you start studying the Seven Rays then you begin to say, 'Ah, yes, I can relate to that, I can resonate with that'.

So, nothing is ever clear cut or simple in the spiritual world, it really isn't. There's no possibility of pigeonholing information in a black and white kind of way. In fact, spiritual understanding is often contradictory because we are dealing with different levels of awareness, of consciousness, of understanding. All of us are created on a specific Ray, one of the seven major Rays. We are created, our seed started on one of those major Rays; and we follow one lifetime through to another fully developing the energy, the quality of that specific Ray, and at the same time each one of us, each soul has to learn to unfold the attributes, the aspects of all the seven Rays.

So, whilst we are one Ray from the moment of creation we still have to go through the lessons and understanding of all the seven Rays and that's where it can get confusing because we can say 'my soul is on the 2nd Ray now,' as we understand it, but it is possible that we were created on the 5th Ray. However, it could be that we have had to go through periods, lifetimes of learning lessons on the 2nd Ray so that we've become so attached to it, so enclosed in it, so enfolded in it that we may think we are 2nd Ray. So, don't close your minds to anything. At one level, we can probably resonate with all the Rays. This may appear confusing but keep your mind open that we have been doing this for many lifetimes and sooner or later we will need to experience all the Rays.

Every Age (e.g. Piscean, Aquarian etc.) lasts roughly 2,400 years and has its own Ray that comes into existence at the beginning of an Age. To try to understand ourselves better, we would need to look at how the Rays affect us by merging the influence of all the different rays which surround us. For example, we could as an individual soul be unfolding our major Ray which might be the 2nd Ray. However, our personality could be the 5th Ray, our mental body could be 3rd, but because the Aquarian Age, (the Age that is currently in manifestation) is actually the 7th Ray, we would need to take the influences of all this and fuse that with the 7th Ray of Aquarius. But remember that all this is done at soul level.

If you have, for example, unfolded a particular Ray to its fullest degree, then it's time perhaps for your soul to start working on another Ray, but that's done at soul level; the understanding and the decisions are made at soul level. Here again, we need to remember group souls and the part we play in our group.

So, who determines then what Ray our seed is on?

In very simple terms, let's go back to our understanding of the beginnings of creation. It has been said by the different teachers and Masters that there was a void, there was darkness and out of the darkness came the Light. It is said that this was accomplished through a series of Divine 'Breaths'. So, let's imagine that the Absolute Being, breathed forth an incredibly powerful Energy and Force from which sound emerged. Perhaps like a hum. It is said that Light and Sound was born out of the void. Then there was the energy, breathed forth, that created the four primary forces of nature, the elements. Then the Creator breathed out this powerful energy seven times This was the creation of the Seven Breaths, the Seven Rays, the Seven Spirits before the throne ~ there's so many ways of describing this, but please take from it whatever seems real and true. The Seven Rays that were breathed into creation all represented a fundamental principle, a quality, an aspect, and above all, an energy. The first three Breaths are the three major Rays.

Definition of the Rays

The first Ray that was breathed forth was the *Ray of Will and Power*. This was Creation. The first Ray creates, but it can also destroy in order to create. This is the active, masculine Ray. It can also be described as the Father.

The second *Ray of Creation is known as Love and Wisdom.* Whilst the first Ray was the active, masculine Ray, the second is the passive feminine Ray. The first Ray could be classified as the Father and the second Ray as the Mother. It needs to be remembered that the first Ray of Will and Power is a tremendous force and on its own can be very destructive because of its incredible power. So, this incredible powerful Ray needs to be tempered by the Love and Wisdom of the passive Mother energy, the Second Ray, which is a gentle, nurturing Ray.

So, the first Ray is the dynamic idea of the Creator, the second Ray is the more passive one. The second Ray formulates the Plan and brings that nurturing aspect into fruition. In other words the first and second Rays are the Father and Mother in unity. The first and second Ray work together to create and nurture.

From the first and second Ray comes the third. The correct name for the third Ray is *Active Intelligence and Adaptability.* These first three Rays can also be described as Father/Mother/Child, Spirit/Soul/Body. The Christian terminology would be, Father/Son/Holy Spirit and again we could also call it the Holy Trinity. Therefore, these are the three major Rays from which the other Rays were born.

The information that has been given out by different sources in the past regarding the Rays and the Masters at the head of each Ray are described below. However, I would point out here that some of the Masters mentioned below may have already moved on to other spheres and, in that case, others will have taken their place.

There are three main positions which oversee the first three major rays. These are:

>The Manu
>The Bodhisattva (Lord Maitreya)
>The Mahachohan (Lord of Civilisation)

Ray 1 – Will & Power – Master El Morya

This is the Ray with the dynamic idea, the powerful energy, the life-force – the Father, Masculine, Active. Because of its powerful energy, it can be both constructive and destructive. It creates and then destroys in order to create.

Ray 2 - Love & Wisdom – Master Kuthumi (or Koot-humi) assisted by the Master Djwhal Khul

This is the Ray that expresses and formulates the Plan; it softens the destructiveness with passiveness and nurturing and with caring – the Mother, passive, nurturing. And out of those two came the third which is:

Ray 3 - Active intelligence and Adaptability – Master R

This is the Ray that takes the Idea and the Plan and puts it into manifestation. So it is the third Ray which is also very powerful and puts everything from the first and second Rays into manifestation.

From the third Ray comes the fourth, fifth, sixth and seventh Rays. These are called the four minor Rays.

Ray 4 - Harmony through Conflict – Master Serapis

This is the Ray which has affected the Piscean Age a great deal. You can imagine the *world- harmony through conflict*. We need to find the peace and harmony within ourselves. This Ray is very prominent in humanity right now and when we look at the conflicts in the world, we can understand why.

Ray 5 - Concrete Knowledge and Science – Master Hilarion

This is the *Ray of the thinker*; this is the Ray that says, 'Yes I hear what you're saying but I need to realize that. I need to *know* it is true.' That's what is meant by concrete knowledge; we *have* to know it within ourselves. It is also known as self-realization because we all know when we realize something in our hearts; we *know* it's true and it doesn't matter what anybody else thinks. It doesn't matter what we may read - if we have realized something within our hearts, that is our understanding of truth. That's concrete knowledge and that is also scientific knowledge. The true scientist brings the light of understanding to the soul.

Ray 6 - Idealism, Devotional and Inspirational – Master Jesus

This Ray has also been very much concerned with the Piscean Age and there's nothing more idealistic and fanatical than the Piscean Age as we have seen in the last 2,000 years. As this Ray is receding, we are currently seeing its energies being perverted into fanatical extremist tendencies manifesting in different parts of the world. But the very positive aspect of this ray is it's quality of deep devotion and altruism.

Ray 7 - Law and Order, Ritual and Ceremonial – was the Master R but now believed to have moved on.

This is the Ray for the Aquarian Age. We are aware that there is law and order in the Universe but it's the freedom of this law and order that the Aquarian age is bringing us. Here I am referring to the natural law and order of the universe. I am not talking about states, nations, legalities, I am talking about the natural law and order of the universe – spiritual law and order. The created universe is a most wonderful creation which has everything in its place and out of that comes the rituals and the ceremonies that can be played out and manifested on the outer levels but there are those on the inner levels too.

Rituals are being played out around us without us being aware of it. Think of the rituals of nature. Think of the rhythm of the seasons and how nature beautifully interacts with the elements and plays out its rituals, season after season.

The Piscean age brought idealism, indoctrination, and conditioning and although we are slowly freeing ourselves, there's still deep within us perceptions and conditioning that we don't always see or understand, unless something happens and we think, 'Why did I react like that?' What happened there? We just don't understand it because we are dealing with so many aspects of ourselves: the emotional body, the mental body, the physical, the spiritual. So whilst we may think emotionally, 'Oh gosh I'm free, I don't have any ties, I don't have any attachments to anything', but the question really is 'what attachments do you have in your mind or emotions? The equal-sided cross is a symbol of balance and freedom. It is the very centre of who we are and all the subtler bodies. That's what we're working towards all the time. That balance – that freedom!

So think of the Rays as an energy, a force that was breathed out in order to create life.

We need to become more and more aware of the dynamic force which is within each one of us. Now one could honestly say, looking at humanity in general, that we all seem to be at the mercy of the forces around us. We are reacting to those forces - that's what's happening in the world today. Nations and individuals are not stopping and saying, 'Hey what's this about? Do we really want to be like this? This is stuff we left behind hundreds of years ago, why are we still continuing doing this?' We are not asking the right questions. We are simply reacting and being caught up in the consciousness that is around us. It is so easy to get caught up in the consciousness prevalent in the masses around us. We really have a great need for detachment and discernment right now at this time of evolution.

So there comes a point when we need to say 'enough' and when we say that, that's when we start the road to freedom. I'm reminded of Nelson Mandela and the long road to freedom and that's exactly what we're doing. The long road to freeing ourselves from past conditioning and indoctrination, but most importantly we really do need to have more soul understanding and soul knowledge. We are now at the point in humanity when the soul is endeavouring to take control, not the personality not the mind, not the emotions; the soul is taking control. It's exciting, it's wonderful; we're no longer materialistic slaves to everything that is going on around us, this is gnosis – and gnosis is knowledge of the inner heart. This is true gnosis.

It's enabling us to find ourselves, within these broader and broader vistas and visions.

When your soul is ready for other knowledge, other information, things will come to you at the right time. This may come through reading a book or meeting a person who may guide you in another direction. You have opened the window of your soul and your soul is ready to take that step towards freedom and knowledge.

Remember the number 7 is an important number; think of the 7 days of Creation. 7 main chakras, the 7 major Rays, then you have the 7 musical notes, the 7 clusters of the Pleiades. The 7 Rays are the seven colours of the spectrum, so the number 7 is a very important number and it all stems back from the 7 major Rays because they were the 7 Breaths and the 7 Spirits before the throne.

The 7 Breaths have their own vibration and all the myriad of forms that were manifested through this sevenfold Breath are probably beyond our comprehension. But remember this is where the ancient symbols come in because, at the time of creation, there was no language as we know it now. It is said that when the Absolute Being breathed the first three Breaths the sacred Word was spoken. The sacred Word again is not as we recognize it, as a word, but rather the AUM, which is also a vibration of the three first major rays:

A the First Ray breathed forth
U the Second Ray breathed forth
M the Third Ray breathed forth

This was the first Sound of creation and here we're talking about millions or trillions of years before the constellations, the planets and the stars were formed. From the void came the Light. How can we with our finite minds try to understand the Infinite?

We are told there is eternity. Eternity means there is no beginning and no end and yet there was a 'beginning' of sorts for when the Creator breathed everything within that great Womb unfolded from potentiality into actuality. As I understand it, with my finite mind, there was a Void (not a vacuum as we know it but a great Unity filled with Intelligence) and through the evolution of energy, vibration, fire, something was formed, something occurred, something breathed so that solid matter came into being. How long did all this last? Well, it is ongoing. There are planets being born continuously, stars exploding and being born. There is no end to it, no 'before' and no 'after'. It seems to me that we cannot fully understand this with the finite mind as the finite mind knows only the things of time, the 'befores' and the 'afters.' We need to wait until we move on to other levels. Trillions and trillions of years.

It is written that chains, schemes, universes came and went. We know of the Cosmos. We know of the Solar System and the Planetary Systems, of Density's and Dimensional levels. We know that this is the 4th round of Earth, that we are in the fifth sub-race of the fifth root-race. But what was there before that? Perhaps these questions may not have answers in a way that our finite mind can understand it – perhaps we will need to wait until we move on to other levels.

The ancient civilizations all had very similar understanding of creation expressed and manifested in different ways, expressed through symbols. They had symbols, but they lived with nature because they understood nature.

Going back to this energy - this vibration that is within ourselves - the seed of our creation may have been created a very long time ago, but the beauty of our spiritual life is that very same seed is within us. It is kept vibrant and that same energy hasn't diminished, it has gained in strength and it will continue to increase as we grow in understanding. Perhaps we need to remember that we are co-creators with the Divine Will and it is this knowledge, this understanding, that will help to lift us out of the imprisonment of the flesh.

Spirit animates matter, so perhaps our breath is Spirit keeping us going. This is the life, the quality and the appearance: Spirit, soul and matter. The life, the quality and the appearance. It's a movement of energy. It's wonderful and absolutely amazing.

We can use all the Rays as they are within us. We may have a major Ray but through many lifetimes we have worked with all the Rays.

One day we will not need the soul, because by then we will have reached the 4th initiation and ascended to a level when we will be the pure essence of Spirit. The soul is necessary, it's the vehicle through which our consciousness evolves and unfolds the soul lessons. However, there will come a time when we will have evolved to the highest degree possible, we will have taken that higher initiation, the fifth, also known as the Great Renunciation or Crucifixion and we will then no longer need the soul. This initiation is about attaining that full

Christ-consciousness. In other words, the soul will have gone through the human experiences and learned the soul lessons to the highest degree possible. It will have overcome the personality, balanced the thoughts and emotions and then it will be therefore ready to move on.

The soul is a vehicle because the Spirit is such a powerful energy, on such a high vibration, that it cannot possibly manifest in the physical body. This body is at present too dense, it needs that transfiguration of a higher consciousness in order to manifest the pure essence of spirit. So, currently it needs the vehicle of the soul consciousness to act as its mediator. The Christ consciousness is so powerful, so strong it could not manifest on earth. When I say the Christ, I am speaking of the Cosmic Christ here, the universal Light. As we know from history, the Christ Consciousness needed a very beautiful vehicle, one that had unfolded and developed through many aeons and had perfected the soul causal body. Over two thousand years ago, the Christ consciousness was able to use the vehicle of the Master Jesus in order to give humanity those beautiful teachings. So it is the same for all of us, our bodies, our physical bodies cannot take that incredible energy of Spiritual essence. Little by little, we take those stepping stones along the path which lead us from one lifetime to another, from one initiation to another, until we reach that glorious height and gain our Christ-like consciousness.

CHAPTER 3

Stepping Stones – Spiritual & Human

What are these stepping stones?

Stepping stones are markers for stepping forward on the spiritual path. The path that a person walks through life is unique. Life itself brings us many opportunities to grow and to unfold. Each one of us has to walk the path alone. In this way we discover our own inner wisdom, our own contact to the Truth within. There are many pathways to choose. How we choose this depends very much on the vibration and quality that is necessary for us individually. We need to trust that each step brings us closer into that greater ocean of life.

It is a path of faith and trust as we totally surrender to the unknown and yet there is something joyous in that surrender and trust. This joy that comes from within is the joy of spirit, the joy of an inner knowing that we are truly much greater than we think we are.

Stepping stones are the soul's awakening, the soul's initiation. The average person seldom thinks of their personal problems, anxieties, and even agonies as having any relation to initiation; but every sorrow, every painful experience is helping your soul towards liberation and to realisation of the Kingdom of Heaven and is therefore infinitely worthwhile.

Some stepping stones at times come in the guise of a crucifixion, however big or small. No doubt these experiences will be painful. We will all go through this in one life or another but yet again this is the path of the soul. Ever learning, ever unfolding, ever striving.

How do we find them?

Each human soul is given the opportunity of following a path of spiritual progression and unfoldment and making ready for its journey to happier climes. This journey is called 'The Path'. It does not begin with incarnation nor end with physical death; it continues onward into the unknown.

We step forward onto another stepping stone when

- We have realized a spiritual truth
- We have reached a deeper understanding
- We have learned something about ourselves
- We have seen clearly some aspect of reality
- We have unfolded another degree in a soul quality
- We have greater vision of the way ahead
- We move from one existence to another

How do they help us?

Stepping stones help us by allowing us to move along the path at our own pace. There is no schedule, no time factor. Only when the soul is ready, when it has realised a truth, and when a lesson has been well and truly learned, then we move on to another stepping stone.

What else do they show us?

- Direction
- Keep us on the straight and narrow
- To see a wider picture
- When we are sometimes precarious – rocky – unsteady
- The way forward
- That when we only look down, we might miss something
- New understanding – new perception

CHAPTER 4

Soul Lessons

What are these?

The journey of the soul takes it through the influence of the twelve signs of the zodiac, expressing and unfolding its spirituality through each one and learning more about its own character The twelve experiences (lessons,) as symbolised mythologically by the twelve Labours of Hercules, represent the sum total of human incarnation. However, it may be that a lesson is not learned to its fullest degree in one lifetime, therefore the soul may need to reincarnate again and again in that particular sign until the lesson has been well and truly learned. We need to learn those lessons on the mental and emotional level.

The soul also goes through different stages of initiation, and particularly the four major initiations related to the four elements of nature. The soul, through many lifetimes is training and preparing itself for the supreme and ultimate initiation in the human evolutionary scheme- this is known as the Christ Initiation – or the attainment of the full consciousness of the Christ Light. Here I need to point out that I am referring to the Christ Consciousness, the Cosmic Light, and not to any individual Master or Being.

Every experience, from the lesser to the greater, has deep significance along the journey. Eventually, through the twelve great labours, the twelve great soul lessons, the soul will overcome and become master of the elements of its nature.

Each soul has a specific quality to unfold during each lifetime. There are twelve great soul lessons *(there are more minor ones too)* but the main twelve great lessons are linked to the signs of the zodiac and the lessons from each sign. This is vast subject and I will write more on this in a further book on the twelve great soul lessons.

It needs to be remembered that all souls have free will. The soul knows its objective, its aim before incarnation and it is at this level that it has free will to choose its path. So, I emphasise, free will is at soul level, not the personality. The soul has a blue-print before it comes into incarnation, but the details of that map are worked out as it travels along the earth journey.

How do we understand these?

We often wish we could understand and know why we have to go through such life experiences as illness, disease, trauma, conflict, relationship issues etc. These life experiences are soul lessons that need to be learned. In understanding these soul lessons, we can play a major part in healing ourselves, through meditation, contemplation and allowing our inner wisdom to guide us.

In rather simplistic terms, we know the physical body is the vehicle for the soul and the soul is the vehicle for pure spirit. We are pure spirit and we chose to enter the Earth planet in order that we may unfold our true nature. It is like the Alpha and the Omega – *I Am (pure spirit)* – *I Know that I Am (spirit having manifested through matter and experienced the lessons of matter)*. The soul holds the pure consciousness of the spirit and it needs to unfold and develop this consciousness through unfolding and developing its many spiritual qualities such as Peace, Tolerance, Patience, Harmony Strength, Courage, Love, Understanding, Truth, Honesty and Integrity.

At this point, we need to remember that every lesson learned at soul level, affects not just us as an individual soul, but also our group soul *(more on group souls in Chapter 5)*. Soul lessons are rich in content and act as catalysts facilitating our development. This may bring about a sense of joy and upliftment in your heart centre. You may be aware of feeling more energetic, happier and healthier. We know that we have made progress when perhaps we are faced with a similar situation or circumstance that may have irked us in the past, but this time, our reaction is very different. We meet this situation or circumstance with more tolerance and understanding. This is because at a deeper level we have learned a soul lesson.

CHAPTER 5

Soul Healing, Soul Understanding

What is meant by this?

Throughout many lifetimes the soul undergoes numerous experiences and challenges in order to develop its spiritual nature. Before birth we are aware of the quality or qualities we need to develop and unfold. We are also aware of any karma that we need to transmute and work upon. We are especially aware of the soul lessons which are necessary for us as an individual souls and also as part of a group soul (*more on this in the following chapter*). It therefore follows that as we grow in understanding, as we accept our experiences, our circumstances, and the memories of past lives, we begin to heal. For some this may be a slow process but for others it may come quite quickly. It is the quality of understanding which is at the root of how we perceive our lives, our experiences and indeed how we perceive others. And it is through understanding that we can heal at all levels.

What is Spiritual Healing?

Spiritual healing is about bringing the soul back into harmony with its inner nature. It is about understanding how to live and work with natural and divine laws. Our true Self, our spirit, is clothed in a number of different bodies each interpenetrating each other and all closely related. In simplistic terms, let us look at the equal sided cross + as an example. At the top, we have the spiritual aspect of ourselves, at the bottom is our physical body (dense matter). One arm is our emotional body and the other arm is the mental body. The ultimate aim of the soul is to balance all these subtler bodies and bring harmony and light to the soul. The very centre of the cross is our heart, the true balance of our spirit.

The greatest problem the soul has is when it allows either the emotions or the mind to take charge and control its life – sometimes it is both! We need to remember that the soul has in its memory, which it brings over from previous lives, recollections of experiences. Some of these experiences were distressing, difficult and often painful. Although in this current life we may not remember these experiences, nevertheless the essence of that memory is still there deep within the soul from one lifetime to another. Some of these recollections play themselves out in our daily lives without us realising. We may have fears, the origins of which are unknown in this current life, but which stem from the memory of a past life. We may have instant dislikes and phobias that we cannot really explain in this life. We may have perceptions and conditioning from the past that affect us now and quite often we are not often aware of these. Both the mental body and the emotional body play on this to gain control and to keep us imprisoned.

What we need to remember is that whatever happened in the past – happened. It cannot hurt us now as we have moved on, we have grown as souls. However, we do reap what we have sown and this is where karma comes in (again more on this in a further chapter). It is by this deep soul understanding that we can free ourselves from the past. This freedom, this releasing and letting go, is what brings balance and harmony into our lives and effectively it is spiritual healing. However, we need to be mindful that it is always wiser to allow the soul to reach back within itself at its own pace. Try not to allow outer influences, which are very prevalent in society nowadays, to influence you into going back within yourself unless your soul is ready. This could have repercussions. It could unleash other memories which your soul is not yet ready to deal with. The quality of wisdom and plain common sense is very important at this stage.

Try to understand that there is a soul purpose behind each ailment. Each illness or disease is only a manifestation on the physical of a soul imbalance. So by balancing the subtle bodies within us, we can truly bring about a spiritual healing. There are many forms or methods of spiritual healing and each one of us has to find the right one which vibrates with our own soul. Again, use wisdom and common sense to discern what is out there available for you and choose the right course to follow.

Healing with the Ancestors

Who are these ancestors? There is a chapter on this further on but simplistically the ancestors play an integral part in our lives whether we are conscious of it or not. They are part of a group soul, our greater Self. They may not necessarily be part of our current family ancestors but in the greater scheme of life, they are our ancestors – this is our spiritual DNA. Each of us is an aspect of a group soul. Therefore, as we learn our lessons, we are enriching the whole group soul. As any other aspect of that group soul are learning their own lessons so are we enriched by their knowledge. This is spiritual law. As above, so below. As below, so above.

What are Chakras or Centres in the Body?

Chakras are centres of light in our bodies through which energy flows. If any of our chakras are blocked this can lead to illness, so it's important to understand what the chakras are about. There are seven main chakras but there are other minor ones. The seven main ones are:

> The **root** (base of spine in tailbone area)
> The **sacral** (lower abdomen area)
> The **solar plexus** (upper abdomen, the stomach area)
> The **heart** (centre of chest, just above the physical heart)
> The **throat**
> The **brow** (third eye chakra) and
> The **crown** (top of head).

The Chakras are linked with the Seven Major Rays (see chapter on Rays). A number of spiritual organisations use colour to help healing the chakras. Colours have a specific quality and it is the essence of this quality that helps that soul to gain understanding of its illness.

To give us a better understanding of how our chakras relate to our everyday lives, below is a chart of the chakras and how it is related to our subtle bodies:

CHAKRA	LINKED TO
Root	Regenerative centre. This is our roots, our foundation, our need to feeling grounded. It is also our ability to re-create. This is a seat of power and the will to be.
Sacral	Our relationship with others. A need to feel nurtured, to feel abundance in our lives.
Solar Plexus	The seat of our emotions. Feelings of resentment, bitterness, hatred, anger and jealousy. Feelings of extreme ecstasy.
Heart	The centre of Love, of inner peace and of joy. Balance, Harmony.
Throat	Our ability to communicate. This is about self-expression, voicing our truth.
Brow	Our third eye chakra when it is fully developed will give us the ability to focus and see the greater picture. The seat of our intuition, imagination and the ability to make decisions based on right thinking.
Crown	The highest chakra represents our ability to be fully connected with our Higher Self – our Spirit – the Monad. Enlightenment.

What are Spiritual Qualities?

The soul journey is to unfold and develop spiritual qualities inherent within. Each lifetime brings us more opportunities for this growth and development. Spiritual qualities represent the essence of Spirit in myriad forms. There are many spiritual qualities. Examples of these are:

ALL ASPECTS OF
LOVE & LIGHT

PATIENCE, TOLERANCE, RESPONSIBILITY, TRUST, COMPASSION, HONESTY, TRANQUILLITY, PEACE, STRENGTH, COURAGE, FAIRNESS, CARING, TENACITY, JOY, HAPPINESS, TRUTH, INTEGRITY, HONOUR, TENDERNESS, GRACE, MERCY, DISCERNMENT, DISCRIMINATION, HOPE, HUMILITY, CHARITY, UNDERSTANDING, HARMONY, DETACHMENT, FORGIVENESS, PERSEVERANCE, FAITH, RESILIENCE, ACCEPTANCE, DETERMINATION, CLARITY, LOYALTY, PURITY, STEADFAST, DEDICATION, RELIABILITY, JUST, MEEKNESS, SWEETNESS, CHASTITY, CONSIDERATE, SINCERITY, SIMPLICITY, GENEROSITY, KINDNESS, HUMOUR W I S D O M

How can Soul Understanding help me to heal myself?

If we are aware and understand what the real issues are behind our problems, our circumstances and our difficulties we can, at soul level, work on ourselves to release whatever it is that is binding us to the past. There are so many methods that we can use, be they affirmations, meditation or working with healing with the Ancestors. We do need to be sensible about this and not try to force understanding or knowledge that our soul is not yet ready to deal with. How do we know this? Be always aware of the Ego, the outer personality, that is still very much attached to the emotional body. Learn to differentiate between the ego and the real soul who speaks to you in order to release you. More on this in a later chapter.

Does healing really work?

Yes, if you approach your soul lessons with pure altruistic motives and, more importantly, if your soul is ready to face its karma and responsibilities. Then, when the lesson is learned, it is like a miracle happening. Throughout many years in healing work I have seen this happen again and again. If we approach our lessons with humility, openness and the willingness to accept our responsibilities for the past and the readiness to move forward, then truly healing can take place. This may appear simple and on one level it is. However, our personality resists and struggles as we try to comprehend what is happening to us. Feelings of resentment, anger and bitterness can creep in but this only adds to the problem. I know it sounds easy to say, but acceptance of your illness is the major first step towards healing. There are also times when the soul goes through illness to allow others around to learn their own soul lessons from their reaction to your illness.

Healing by Colour

There are some methods of spiritual healing which use colour to heal patients. Colour is known to have qualities and it is the quality attributed to these colours which resonates with the soul of the patient. The following examples may be of interest:

GOLD – a colour that will uplift a patient, bringing joy and sunshine
BLUE – a colour of peace, stilling the mind and emotions
GREEN – the colour of nature, bringing balance, cleansing, clearing
ROSE – the colour of love
AMETHYST – the colour of wisdom
VIOLET – the colour of deep understanding
RED – a powerful colour, to be used wisely, bringing vitality
ORANGE – a colour that brings energy

CHAPTER 6

Group Souls

What is meant by a group soul?

A group soul consists of individual souls – call them aspects – that are linked together on a major Ray. It is said that there could be as little as ten aspects in a group soul but possibly more. The group soul purpose is to unfold and develop the qualities of that Ray through the unfoldment, development and experiences gained from successive lifetimes. Group souls work as a unit to develop and manifest a quality or qualities and they attain initiation as a group. All aspects of that group soul work on a similar vibration.

Each aspect, each individual soul can take on different incarnations to unfold their own individual soul qualities yet, at the same time, they are also helping their group soul with the major purpose attributed to their specific Ray. Group souls are linked to a particular major Ray but will also be developing on other Rays.

Aspects of a group soul can incarnate separately or some may choose to come together to support each other through life's experiences. This is where we often have families that are closely linked together and form part of an ancestral group soul. Other aspects may choose to come alone, possibly in conditions which are alien to them, in order that their soul may grow in strength and courage and other soul qualities that need unfoldment.

At every stage, the experiences and the lessons learned through the successive incarnations are all linked to the group soul and therefore what we learn individually helps to enhance the unfoldment and development of the group soul. Thus, when we hear the saying that we are never alone, it is a very true one. We may often feel alone physically, emotionally and mentally, and it is often painful to go through conditions without the companionship of another to help bear the pain and experience, but if only we could really understand that all aspects of our group soul are with us all the way. As we learn, they learn. As they learn, we learn.

There are group souls who have an important work to perform in the service of humanity. There are many fields of service. At times, some aspects of the group soul may be in incarnation and other aspects may be in spirit, guiding and supporting those on Earth. Often, they are known as guides and helpers. If a group soul has a very important mission to perform, then they usually come under the guidance of a Master or a disciple of the Master. It is worth remembering that it is the discarnate souls who have the wider vision and are best able to see the goal clearly.

To understand what a group soul is we need to be aware of the following:

A group soul has a group consciousness; a group awareness; a group purpose

How do the above express or manifest?

It expresses itself primarily through the:

- Soul ray
- Initiation
- Soul Lessons
- Soul Qualities
- Root-race

How are these factors manifested?

- Through our individual lives
- Through our chakras
- Through our health

- Through the culture we live in
- Through the nation we live in

What is Group Soul Recognition?

Throughout life we encounter many people with whom we feel a great affinity and know that at some level we seem to have known each other before. Often we just smile and acknowledge the bond but we don't truly understand how that can be when we know that, at the physical level, we have not met before. Sometimes that recognition is all there is, as it is obvious that our lives are very different and there is really very little contact that follows. Yet, at other times, there is such a connection and the bond is so strong that we know without question that that person is very much part of us but perhaps we don't understand how.

Equally we can meet people for the first time and we react with an instant dislike and, in some cases, just want to get away from them as quickly as possible. Yet in reality we know that since we have just met them they have never physically harmed us in any way but the feeling is still there. Sometimes we subjugate first impression feelings by saying to ourselves that we are just being silly and give that person the benefit of the doubt. However, sooner or later in a relationship we often find ourselves in a situation where we remember that initial reaction and then we know that our gut, or initial first impression, may have been right after all. The obvious possibility is that there is past karma between us and therefore that needs to be transmuted.

So, why this reaction?

We need to know and remember at this point that there are different degrees of recognising and acknowledging an old bond.

In the first instance, our soul has recognised a kindred spirit. Perhaps someone with whom we have had an association in a previous lifetime and it has obviously been a good association for that warm recognition.

Secondly, when the bond appears stronger, then this soul has been in a closer relationship with us, whether it be a family association, or belonging to a similar fraternity, or neighbours or such like. These associations have been much more on an emotional or a mental level.

Thirdly, there is a much deeper soul recognition and that is when we recognise another aspect of our group soul.

How can we tell the difference?

- By observing your reaction
- By allowing your intuition its freedom
- By allowing your higher mind to discern between these reactions

What about those we meet whom we dislike instantly?

It is very possible, actually highly likely, when one considers how many lives we have had, that throughout different incarnations we may have had an unfortunate or negative encounter with another soul on the path. They could be on another Ray or indeed they could be on our own particular Ray of our group soul. If the encounter has been painful, whether on the emotional, physical or mental level, this has been registered at the soul level, and therefore there is a soul memory recognition, although we don't of course necessarily remember what happened before.

Karmic responsibilities

On whatever level, if there has been negative reaction and there is karma to be learned and transmuted, then souls are brought together, again and again until the lesson has been truly learned and forgiveness has taken place. This is where the wonderful soul qualities of forgiveness and detachment play a unique part in transmuting karma. Always remembering that karma is not a punishment but simply an opportunity to learn.

When we truly understand and learn about soul qualities, when we see that each happening and situation in our lives is bringing us closer to that ultimate truth, we can find the forgiveness in our hearts to let go and acknowledge that we are all just souls on the spiritual path, all aspects of a greater soul.

So, in a sense what I am saying here, and this may appear contradictory to what I have said before, is that if we understand at soul level why another individual has harmed us in whatever shape or form, then there is no need for forgiveness, because the soul has understood. The soul has realised that the other soul is just like us, walking through life's journey, learning, unfolding, falling and picking ourselves up. They are no different from us so as we give ourselves that deep soul level understanding, natural law determines that we give another this understanding so *no hurt is acknowledged* – ergo no forgiveness necessary! Another stepping stone forward. Another lesson learned.

What is a Soul Mate?

A soul mate is another aspect of our group soul with whom we have a fundamental soul link, i.e. developing the same soul qualities, linked to the same soul Ray. We could meet several aspects of our soul group within an incarnation and feel tremendous links with them. This is different to linking with an aspect, or rather another soul, with whom we have had close ties in previous incarnations. The bond here would not be as strong.

What is a Twin Soul?

A twin soul is an aspect of our duality, whilst we are living in the realm of dualities. What do I mean by duality? We are both male and female, negative and positive, yin and yang in one. Each aspect needs to feel complete on its own. Sometimes we may need to find our 'twin soul' to develop certain qualities of the soul together. Here, we can either incarnate in male or female bodies. But I repeat, each aspect, whether male or female, needs to be complete on its own, to develop and grow to full consciousness. Often, we need to go it alone with our 'twin soul' supporting and guiding us from another realm of consciousness. It is very possible that in some lifetime we may meet our twin soul. However, it doesn't always follow that we should be together. Awareness of responsibilities is so important here.

How to recognise a Soul Mate/Twin Soul?

- A soul who does not need or wish to control us
- Who allows us space, not due to indifference, but out of love and respect for our growth
- A true heart link
- One that knows, understands, accepts and loves us as we are

Remember that our soul mate/twin soul is also developing and growing spiritually as we are and will have their contribution to make towards the group soul. There are different aspects of growth – perhaps on another level of consciousness or perhaps vibrating to a different Ray.

It is worth remembering our responsibilities along the path.

What is the Ancestral Group Soul?
Knowing Our Ancestors – Our Spiritual DNA

When we speak of our spiritual DNA, we are not just speaking of our earthly ancestors, of our current family history. We are speaking of our Ancestral Group Soul. This is the history of our soul. Being part of an ancestral group soul takes us beyond the immediate family history. Indeed, some people feel very little connection with their earthly family whilst others know that there is a deep affinity between them. On both counts we may have taken on continued group karma. It takes us back to where we originally came from. It takes us back to the very impulse that created us. We are all aspects of a greater Group Soul. It is the Group Soul that knows the Plan, the greater Plan. The Group Soul knows its objective and creates the circumstances for each individual aspect to incarnate to continue the journey of self-discovery.

So how do we define the Ancestral Group Soul? How is it made up? To understand this, we need to remember that there are many facets to a Group Soul. We need to be aware of the Planetary life, the Ray on which we have been created, the life-stream, the root-race, what initiation (whether human or planetary) we are experiencing, what soul lessons we are learning and what spiritual qualities we are unfolding.

By embracing all these, it could lead us to the conclusion that our ancestors live through us as it is a natural progression of evolution. As aspects of something greater than ourselves, as we evolve, as we learn and unfold our own spiritual qualities, so are the Ancestral Group Soul unfolding and learning too. This means that through us our Ancestral Group Soul continues its journey through one lifetime after another. If this is so, perhaps the next question to ask is: Are we our ancestors and will our descendants be us? Is this then the eternal life? It seems that we continue, albeit in different bodies, but the soul memory, the consciousness continues to evolve and grow until we reach that point of the Omega, *I Know that I Am*.

With the realisation of there being something greater than ourselves, we could also realise that perhaps a condition or health problem has manifested because of a soul dis-harmony, lessons unlearned in previous lives. If we accept that we are all part of an Ancestral Group Soul, could our problem or condition be taken back to our Group? What understanding can we derive from all this? Wise teachers tell us that all diseases are a manifestation of soul dis-ease, a soul dis-harmony. Therefore, we need to go back to our Ancestral Group Soul to try to figure it out.

Our spiritual DNA is not about our physical bodies on a molecular and cellular level. It is about understanding our ancestry at soul and spiritual level. It is about the understanding of *who we are* and *what part we play* in the unfolding purpose of humanity. Our lives are not just about 'plain little me', our lives are integrated with something far greater than ourselves. If this is so why are we not aware of this? Very simply, it is the experience of our lives and conditions that is enabling our Group Soul to evolve. There are other aspects too developing and unfolding through our own experience which enrich the whole Group. If we knew or were aware of others, then our reaction to our experiences would be influenced by that knowledge. As individual souls we only progress by our own reaction to experiences and how we deal with them.

So our contact with the ancestors and our quest for our spiritual DNA lies in the acceptance and acknowledgment that there is something far greater than 'little me'. Once we realise and understand the depth of our very being, acknowledging the presence of the ancestors is not so difficult. The difficulty lies with the 'outer mind' letting go.

To honour our ancestors, we must first honour ourselves. Not just as the individual we see in the mirror each day, but as the soul that is behind the Light shining from our eyes. It is this acceptance of the soul that will eventually help us to recognise our true being. It is this understanding that will eventually give credence to the essence of our being. This understanding, this knowledge comes with self-realisation. We may read many books, go to many lectures and workshops and listen to many teachers and we may acquire knowledge of the mind, but until we have realised *Truth* in our hearts, we will never really 'know' – this is our inner knowledge - this is gnosis.

It is through the soul memory that we can contact the Ancestral Group Soul. The ancestors are there to help us. Through their own experiences, they have given us many gifts, many qualities. We live with these gifts and these qualities in our everyday lives, but we may not be aware of this. These are our spiritual genes. What we do with them is up to us. It is our own experiences that enhance these genes. As we develop and unfold our spiritual qualities through the lessons we learn from everyday life, so are we enriching the very essence of our Ancestral Group Soul. When we begin to realise that the soul is who we truly are, we also realise that the personality is not an enemy to our growth. The personality is the servant of the soul; it is the vehicle through which the soul can express itself. The more we allow this to happen, the more that we are expressing our divinity in the world.

We are not separate from the Creator, we are rather integral aspects of the Absolute – we are potentially (to the degree that we use our freewill aright) co-creators with the Divine Will. Our enlightenment does not come as a gift from God; it comes from our well-earned lessons throughout our soul's journey and history. Enlightenment means becoming the radiant divine Self that we are, once we have shed the cloak of the personality and recognised and acknowledged the spiritual essence within.

Our motivation comes with the knowledge that we are eternal; that there has never been a time when we have not been spirit. In this realisation we can take comfort from the fact that whatever life may throw at us, we have the inner depth, the inner strength to cope and overcome.

This is a time when humanity is awakening. It is awakening to its true potential, to a spiritual dimension deep within. It may not always understand or know what that potential is, but it senses that although we are all unique, we are all part of a greater life. The Soul of humanity is awakening to its real '*I Am*', to its real consciousness. We are awakening to our collective soul – a Group Soul. It has learned through its history of collective experiences; it has expressed itself through different races, religions and cultures and it is now awaiting its moment to sense, through the miasma of human diversity, that inner unity. It is through the richness of our differences, our diversity that we will recognise who we are and unite in true brotherhood.

The Soul of humanity is seeking to inculcate a higher set of values into us. Whilst this is a period of real painful adjustments for so many, it is also a time when humanity is entering into a more enlightened period. This is a time when we can measure ourselves by how we deal with crisis and conflict. It was Martin Luther King who said: *'The ultimate measure of a man is not where he stands in moments of convenience, but where he stands in moments of challenge, in moments of great crisis and controversy.'*

So how can we support the Soul of humanity? How can we live up to that higher potential, those higher values? How can we fulfil our destiny, our purpose?

We can support humanity's oneness by honouring diversity. We can be tolerant and understand that there is a dual purpose behind all happenings - the spiritual and the material - that is the soul and the personality. Let us look at people and at world events with a dual eye. Everything has a purpose – nothing happens by chance. World conditions, crisis is all part of the journey. The living soul of earth is also growing.

In order that we can do this, we need to look beyond the outer form, beyond the personality, to sense the truth that the soul conceals. It would be prudent to remember that not one individual, nor one nation, nor one religion has found the one Truth, but each has found a pathway to it.

When we begin to understand, and see duality, we will get away from black and white, from good and evil. Instead we realise that in everything there is a mixture of both.

Humanity has entered a great period of crisis on the road to enlightenment and freedom. We are facing enormous challenges and yet this is not a time to either show fear or despair about our future. It is merely a period of more testing and lessons to be learned. We are going forward from one great Age (Piscean) to another (Aquarian). Huge changes need to take place. Old structures need to be dismantled. This will be scary for many. Truly 'things ain't what they used to be' and if this is right, we cannot progress on old agendas nor old structures. We do need to refrain from 'throwing out the baby with the bath water'. Everything has its own rhythm, its own time and time will not stand still.

The Soul of humanity – our great Group Soul is moving forward and seeking greater expression in the material world. This is truly a time of transformation, a great awakening in the history of souls. We all have the responsibility to play our part. We can do this with courage, with understanding and above all with unconditional love.

We go back and reiterate that our ancestors play an integral part in our lives whether we are conscious of this or not. That we all belong to a Group Soul and often we may have close ties, links with relatives because we are all part of that same Group Soul. However, let us remember when we speak of the Ancestral Group we are not just speaking of physical family ancestors but rather of a larger Group Soul connected to our own soul Ray. Being part of an Ancestral Group Soul takes us beyond our immediate family history.

So who are our Ancestors and what part do they play in our lives?

It is worth remembering that

WE ARE WHO WE ARE BECAUSE OF WHO THEY WERE

However, we are not necessarily WHAT we are because of WHAT they were.

So what is the difference between WHO and WHAT?

        WHO   - SOUL
        WHAT   -PERSONALITY

Group Ancestral Soul – So Who are they?

Our Ancestors live through us – there is a natural progress of evolution through the Group Soul. In other words, they are us and we are them. Our Ancestral Group Soul continues its journey through successive lifetimes and therefore our ancestors and descendants are all part of this group soul. Each successive lifetime we may come in different bodies, different families, different cultures or races. Nevertheless the Group Soul is ever learning, ever growing, ever developing.

We may wish to contact the Ancestral Group Soul to link with our past, not to cling on to issues but rather to resolve them, heal ourselves and move on.

To grasp, to even an infinitesimal degree, what an Ancestral Group Soul is, we need to understand how it is made up, or rather what defines the Ancestral Group Soul?

The ancestral group soul is defined by:

- Planetary Life (The life of the Planetary Logos in actuality right now). The Planetary Logos is a centre in the body of the Solar Logos who in its turn is a centre in the body of the Cosmic Logos). This is a very simplistic way of describing the hierarchy of Universal Life. The Planetary Logos could also be described as the God in orthodox Religion.

- Soul Ray (one of the Seven Major Rays of Creation)
- Life Stream (human, devas, angelic)
- Root Race (We are in the fifth sub-race of the fifth root race. The previous races were Polarian, Hyberborean, Lemurian, Atlantean)
- Initiation (Human, Planetary)
- Soul Lessons
- Soul Qualities

So that we may learn more about our Ancestral Group Soul, we need to understand what Group Souls are.

Our family ancestors, especially if they are part of that greater Group Soul, are also unfolding through us, for we are all aspects of that one Group Soul. It would be lovely and neat if we could truly say that we all accomplish everything our soul's blue-print requires of us in one lifetime, but for the vast majority of us, we do not manage to cross all the 't's and dot all the 'i's'. The beauty of the path of the soul is that there are no time restrictions and because there is no ending, one lifetime follows another and the lessons learned, or yet to be learned at soul level, have successive lifetimes to be realised. Everything is in constant motion.

How do we do this?

The outer life inevitably brings responsibilities and some of these may conflict. For those on the spiritual path, there will be a recognition of sacrifices having to be made for the greater good. For most people it is almost impossible to recognise the difference between the sacrifice for the individual or that for the group soul. Thereby we end up with great conflicts and confusion. Because of this, disease, soul dis-ease or dis-harmony, may manifest in the physical body.

So we now come to a point where we need to understand and differentiate between the two responsibilities. So, what does this mean?

We reach a stage in our spiritual path, when we truly attain deeper understanding of ourselves, even if this may not always be apparent to the outer mind. The soul knows, the soul always knows. There may be lifetimes when the need or desire of the individual soul needs to surrender to the needs of the Group Soul. How do we know this? Perhaps the soul is very certain of a path it wants to follow, however, life's circumstances may not allow this to happen. This can bring frustration and maybe even resentment to the individual. A simple explanation would be that the individual needs to stay in those peculiar and perhaps sometimes difficult circumstances until a lesson has been learned for the Group Soul.

How does this knowledge become apparent?

Our everyday lives give us more information than we realise. Our reactions, our thoughts, our aspirations, all serve to bring us closer to that connection with our soul consciousness and slowly we allow our soul to direct our lives. But this can take time because we don't always truly understand ourselves or the path along which our soul is guiding us.

However, our ancestors live through us. This may be astonishing to you but it is a natural progress of evolution for the Ancestral Group Soul.

If we have a strong link with other family members, then it is truly worth listening to the snippets of family history about our ancestors. We may hear tales of characteristics regarding our grandparents or great-grandparents. By listening, by discerning what we hear and by trying to relate that to our own lives and even possibly a health issue, we can understand or see a thread, a link coming down the ancestral line. By following these steps we can reach a level of contact, understanding and awareness that will help us to grow spiritually and at the same time allow the Ancestral Group Soul to continue its unfoldment and development on the spiritual path. This knowledge, this understanding may help us to heal a genetic condition. Every physical condition is a manifestation of a soul dis-harmony. If this runs in a family, then we can trace it back and try to heal this.

Why do we have genetic health problems?

If we can accept that all physical diseases are a manifestation of a soul dis-ease, then it would be a natural progression to accept that:

*Any soul quality which any aspect of our
Ancestral Group Soul still needs to
develop will continue to present itself to us
through successive lifetimes until
that soul quality has been well and truly
unfolded and lesson learned.*

Therefore, this would affect our health, our thoughts and our emotions.

This means that through us our Ancestral Group Soul continues its journey through one lifetime after another. It would be true to say that we are our ancestors and our descendants will be us.

The question arises, if our health problem is about a soul dis-ease, and we can in a family history trace back health problems, what can we do to heal ourselves and at the same time heal our Ancestral Group Soul?

The answer may be to try to connect with our ancestors by attunement or meditation and bring clarity and understanding to our current problems or health conditions.

Our ancestors are always willing and happy to help; it is up to us to try to make this contact and call on them for help to heal ourselves.

It is necessary at this stage to remember our karmic responsibilities. Whilst healing ourselves is of course beneficial to us personally, we need to be aware that we are also dealing with group karma and we need to be responsible and in some ways sacrificial in how we deal with the problem.

It is this knowledge, this understanding and this awareness of something greater than ourselves that will help us to reconcile our current lives with our life-stream and allow us to experience the magnitude of *who* we are, so that we can, with deep altruism, understanding and knowledge, not only help to heal ourselves but also help our Ancestral Group Soul to learn and evolve.

We will now take, one by one, the different aspects which make up the Ancestral Group Soul.

8) What Is Healing with the Ancestors? How can we Heal Ourselves?

As has been said previously in this book, the Ancestral Group Soul is made up of facets or aspects and develops along the planetary life, the Ray, on which it was created. It also unfolds along the life-stream, the root-race and the initiation it is experiencing. Moreover, it expresses the soul lessons and the spiritual qualities it is unfolding. As each aspect or facet develops, the understanding, purpose and quality of the whole group is building and unfolding the knowledge of the Ancestral Group Soul.

Individually, as our chakras or centres develop, it unfolds the understanding, purpose and quality of our individual soul antahkarana. This is the bridge that connects the lower to the higher (the personality to the soul, and the soul to the spirit). The antahkarana gives us deeper insight, something that the outer mind, the personality, may not always be able to fathom. We need to realise that there is a soul purpose behind each ailment. So what is that purpose and how can we find this out?

To try to discover that purpose we need to be very clear and honest with ourselves. We all have deep connections with the Ancestral Group Soul. The connection goes back aeons; therefore the current problem or condition may also go back some time, through successive lifetimes. Our ancestors are willing to help us to understand so that we may, in our own time, learn how to deal with and heal the condition or problem that we may be facing. With knowledge also comes deep responsibility. There needs to be a very specific purpose and intention in our meditative process. Remember too that all conditions have a deeper soul meaning. We can try to link and work with the ancestors and ask for their help. Here is a simple meditative process that may help you. Start by asking yourself these questions:

- Why do you want to do this?
- Would you find it really helpful – for yourself or a loved one?

- Have you ever felt a connection to an Ancestral Group?
- What is the current problem?
- Is it physical, mental, emotional, spiritual?
- Have you ever been conscious that you belong to something far greater than yourself?
- Have you ever been conscious of helpers, guides, angels?
- Can you feel a connection or can you relate to an ancestor?
- Have you ever been aware of a presence – a gentle guidance?
- What kind of help do you want?
- How can you bring clarity and understanding to a current problem?
- Is it a genetic disease?
- Is it a family repetitive pattern?
- Is it affecting other family members?
- Can you go beyond the medical/scientific reasoning?
- Can the current problem be related to a particular chakra?

We need to remember:
- That there may be deeper soul responsibilities.
- Be respectful and aware of sacred space and contracts at soul level
- Honour the ancestors
- Accept your place in that Group Soul
- Give thanks to them
- Be open to receive
- Be willing to co-operate
- Be willing to change
- Be understanding. Our family ancestors were also doing their best
- Our ancestors do not want us to stay stuck/trapped in the past
- No guilt, no blame, just the need to acknowledge, to accept, to heal and move on

So here is a suggestion for a simple meditative process:
Preparation time:

- Start by writing down what your purpose is in wanting to call upon the ancestors
- Prepare yourself physically
- Prepare yourself emotionally and mentally
- Prepare your space
- Switch off phones, make sure you will not be disturbed
- Be very clear as to your intention
- Don't ask for too many things at once – just concentrate on one at a time
- Start by breathing in and out gently
- Slowly and gently attune yourself to the Light
- Raise your awareness to that centre of peace and stillness within you
- Then, when you are feeling at peace and still centered:
- Ask for your guide or guardian angel to be present to help you
- Feel their strong support around you, then:
- Ask and invite the ancestors to join you
- Allow this to happen naturally
- When you feel or see a presence ask for help and understanding about your problem
- Wait – let go of all pre-thoughts and requests
- Accept whatever comes
- When you feel that enough has been done for one day, then:
- Give thanks to the 'ancestor', 'helper'
- Give thanks overall for the guidance and protection received
- Use the gentle in and out breath to become aware of the physical body and your surroundings

It's important to be aware that our ancestors may only be able to show us symbolically what they are trying to share. Please do not get upset if nothing appears to be clear or indeed if nothing is happening. There are always reasons for this. Perhaps we are too anxious and thereby putting up blocks *(even if we may not be aware of this)*. We need also to be aware that our interpretation of what we have been given may be clouded by our own sub-conscious or perception.

The essential thing is that you have asked. In their own time, when you least expect it, the answer will come.

CHAPTER 7

Spiritual Freedom

What is meant by this?

Throughout many lifetimes over aeons of years, we have at one point or another been under the influence of orthodoxy. This can be in the form of religion, tribal belief, culture, or planetary age. In other words, we are born under the thumb of indoctrination, conditioning and perception. Our feelings and our thoughts may be influenced by all these but it is possible that deep within there is a stirring of wanting to be free – some may call it wanting to be a 'free spirit'. Spiritual freedom is not so much about freeing ourselves from any of these things, but rather comes about when we at long last truly recognise and understand that we are primarily spirit, and that spirit is seeking to manifest its essence and energy through the physical. At this point, all that has been so important on the physical level, be it emotional or mental, fades away and we now have before us a purpose, an understanding that we had not appreciated before. It may not necessarily mean that all our circumstances or conditions fade away but rather that we approach them from the essence of spirit and not from the personality. Spiritual freedom is about getting in touch with the real 'I' within, and living and walking our 'talk'.

What is Indoctrination, Conditioning, Perception?

In so many ways, these three have kept us imprisoned for a very long time. From the moment we are born we are indoctrinated into the habitual beliefs and perceptions of our families, the communities in which we live, and perhaps our religious communities too. These beliefs also inevitably extend to the cultures of which we are part, the race and also the nation in which we live. Usually we are not aware of this as children and some may never recognise that indoctrination exists, or refuse to believe that in this day and age we could be indoctrinated. For others, there is the recognition that their reactive thinking and feeling are not their own and by deduction they realise that it was their parents or grandparents thinking or the culture or nation itself, which influenced them so much. Those generations lived from the truth that they knew at the time, but life has changed and we have moved on. Life and society has developed. Once again we really do need to remember that this is not about apportioning blame on anyone or on society. It is how they were with the knowledge they had.

How do we free ourselves?

It is worth asking ourselves – is this my thinking? Is this how I truly feel? Or am I just following a pattern, a habitual belief from the past? When this questioning happens, then we begin to take steps forward to freeing ourselves. Slowly, we continue that questioning in a detached manner. It is necessary not to put any blame on our parents, or grandparents. That was their belief, they did their best. But now it is our time for asking. This now becomes our quest. Our soul is taking us along another stepping stone into spiritual freedom. We see things differently, we live in today's society.

What is meant by Consciousness?

Consciousness is a knowing, it is an accumulation of our soul's experience. Consciousness is the soul's insight throughout its journey and the experiences it has undertaken. This insight develops as we journey along the path. We retain the memories of our soul lessons in our consciousness – it is like a storehouse where the soul memory of all the lessons learned throughout lifetimes is gathered for us to consider and understand. Consciousness is that part of ourselves that knows deep down when something is true. This is our guiding light. On the outer, mental or emotional, we don't know why this is true, but if we are attuned well enough to our soul, we know this is truth. Consciousness is an inner-knowing, a sum total of all that we have ever experienced.

What is meant by Awareness?

Throughout our lives, there comes a moment when we can suddenly become aware of something that is quite subtle, so subtle maybe that we cannot define it but yet we know it to be tangible. Awareness comes when we have had an inner realisation, a soul recognition of a truth. Something that has touched us deeply and awakened something within our soul memory. This can also be referred to as inner knowledge. We may go through many lifetimes asleep to the spheres of the spirit, but then suddenly one lifetime, we become aware of something inside, something that tells us there is more. When our awareness is awakened, we want to know more and more. Our awareness is also our awakening from the slumber. Once awakened, this awareness stays with us and gradually over time and, if we don't dismiss it as just being vague, it is this awareness of something more than ourselves that will push us forward, that will help us to strive for more knowledge, more understanding.

How Do We Know the Difference Between Intuition and Our Imagination?

What is Intuition?

Intuition comes from deep within ourselves. The words in-tuition derives from our inner teacher, our soul, our spirit. It is our inner selves, our highest selves teaching and reminding us of an inner truth, an inner clarity, an inner knowing. As we unfold our spirituality, as we become more and more aware of who we truly are, then we have the confidence to listen to our inner teacher and above all to accept what it is trying to teach us. So often in life, there comes a flash of knowing, an understanding that we can't quite explain, we are so certain - we just know! This is our intuition, it makes itself known perhaps fleetingly at first but as we grow in confidence, as we grow in understanding of the world of spirit, we begin to trust it. Trusting our intuition is so necessary on the spiritual path but also can be so confusing. At first, we doubt ourselves, we ask is this intuition or does it come from my imagination, my personality's ego. Only time and working on ourselves will bring us that absolute trust. And it does come. Perhaps slowly and at times even painfully, but it does come! Follow your intuition because this comes from your inner teacher, your spirit. This then is your Truth.

What is Imagination?

Imagination is of the outer mind. Often when we start meditating the imagination can really play havoc and produces all kinds of imagery. However, it can also help us to visualise, to create a scenario which can uplift us for a while. It is important though to remember that we do not perceive imagination to be real but rather use it as a tool to help us with our meditation and contemplation. Imagination is wonderful as it can uplift us and for a while we can lose ourselves in this. But imagination can also deceive us. It can do this through our personality's ego. We can really run riot with this and this is fed by our mind and our emotions. On the spiritual path, we are often told to be wary of the grandiose imagery that we think we have been given. Perhaps in our imagination we believe that in our meditation we have been given signs or symbols that may imply we have been an exalted Being in the past or we are now under the tutorship of a Master or such like. The truth is that sometimes we are shown an image of a Master or exalted Being to simply indicate the era of the past where we may have had a life. It could also be that we are shown the image of a Master simply because we are unfolding on that specific ray. There are many explanations that can be given in meditations. What can we make of this, what can we believe? Very simply, observe what you have seen or been given, no doubt the information is interesting, and just 'park it' or write it down. Perhaps at a later time, when we have learned more about the spiritual path and gained more wisdom, we may have a very different interpretation.

How Do We Aspire to A Higher Level?

As we travel the spiritual path, there comes a time when we have to face certain realities about ourselves in greater depth, particularly as we aspire to a higher consciousness, these could be defined as:

HONESTY – no punches pulled
FEAR – based on lack of understanding
PRIDE – which veils your vision
SPIRITUAL ARROGANCE- which is the greatest SIN and great stumbling block
COURAGE – which comes only through inner strength, inner understanding
DISCRIMINATION – the real difference between the ways of earth and the ways of the spirit
HUMILITY – which comes with greater awareness and understanding and a true willingness to serve
DETACHMENT – a necessary quality to develop on the spiritual path
TRUST – without trust, we can have no faith nor hope
PREJUDICE – a stain against our humanity

These are in no specific order as all these are inter-related and therefore necessary for us to face on the spiritual path. If we wish to truly aspire to the highest within, then we should be prepared to face the WHOLE that is us. There are so many pitfalls that can beset us when we set out feet on the path of enlightenment. These are facets of our personality which serve to teach us more about ourselves so before we reject them or feel bad if we are conscious of having one or more of these aspects, do remember that it is through the personality, through the human aspect that spirit can express itself.

Let us now take each of the above facets in greater detail bearing in mind that we can all enlarge upon it with our own individual experiences.

HONESTY

This is an aspect which probably requires a lot of courage and wisdom. We so often say that we are willing to face realities and truths about ourselves and to a certain degree this may be true, but we are not really aware how much pride we have until we start digging deep down and start coming face to face with our weaknesses.

To face ourselves honestly, we need to strip ourselves right down and stand naked before the Mirror of Truth. It is so easy to admit to little weaknesses and we do this at times with a touch of pride at our own endeavours in this search. But this search for honesty does not stop as soon as we have stripped off the first layer, it must be kept on if we wish to go forward on the path. The first layers to come off are probably the easiest to admit and face. Then the going gets tougher as, with true motivation, we keep digging.

How should we dig? How do we find out the truth about ourselves?

There is no greater Teacher nor mirror than our fellow-men. It is by searching for ourselves in others that we find ourselves. This may be difficult and hard to grasp at first and very often painful. For so often we kid ourselves that we are not at fault when others mistreat us or upset us. But when we dig deep and develop the quality of HONESTY we will realise that every time someone makes us irritable, angry or upset or hurts us, it is because they are showing us an aspect of ourselves which we do not like. It is so easy to deceive ourselves that we have given no or little provocation or justification for this hurt. But all pain comes from that within us that we need to face and release.

To be HONEST is to be prepared to look at our own weaknesses, shed a few tears if necessary or if it helps you, for by doing this you are allowing that release, which is keeping the real you imprisoned. In this voyage of self-discovery our emotions will be greatly stirred and it is then that we need to keep that inner light constant and polarised.

We will discover much about ourselves that perhaps we were not even aware of. One of the biggest shocks we may encounter is the realization of how much self-pride we possess. It is so easy to delude ourselves. We are so willing to admit to little weaknesses but when we are suddenly faced with a self-Truth that we have always found abhorring in others, it is like finding ourselves naked in front of a mirror, yet again. And this realization can come as a great shock. None of us think we are perfect, but it is comfortable to think of ourselves with the imperfections that we like to have and because we are aware of these little imperfections we feel we are honest about ourselves.

But this is only part-honesty. To be really honest is to want to willingly stand naked in front of the mirror of truth the mirror that is reflected to us by our fellow-men. And when that mirror no longer upsets or shocks us or gives us pain, when you can look and accept each gesture from your brethren without flinching, then you can say you have found HONESTY.

Along the stepping stones of my spiritual path I have found the following mantram very helpful. I share this with you:

LOVE, LIGHT & PEACE

I use it when I am doing my breathing exercises each day.

On the intake of, I think   LOVE, LIGHT
And on the out-breath, I think   AND PEACE

FEAR

What is the real meaning of fear? We so often think of fear as something that would terrorises us, that might upset our equilibrium in the physical sense. There are many types of FEAR. There are fears of the physical of violence in one form or another; there are fears of the emotions – which affects us at the solar plexus area; and there are fears of the mind which can cause us incredible anxiety, worry, stress Then there is the fear that exists based on our own perception which is based on our conditioning of life and all it illusions and glamour. One could say that the fears of a western individual is very different to that of an easterner or other cultures. We pick up, as children, the fears of our families and of the society we live in.

Fear comes from within. And we fuel this fear within us by our lack of understanding, by our constant feeding it with ignorance. Fear is based on our ignorance. Fear is based on our unwillingness to reach clarity of what is real and what is unreal. We so often accept our conditioning, our indoctrination without questioning and we are afraid to stand up and find truth for ourselves. So we remain in ignorance which breeds fear.

But this refusal to search for the Truth is what holds us back from reaching the highest. We are afraid to release and let go of those things that are familiar to us because in a way they measure up to our security. We are afraid to let go of people even if perhaps they have nothing further to offer us. We may not always understand that karma may be over and we need to move on. We are afraid to overcome and release the emotions because we prefer to believe those emotions is love. We keep binding ourselves to our possessions because we believe they are important to our comfort and security. In other words we are afraid to change because in changing we would lose the comfortable "I", the outer self that has dominated our lives for so long.

We keep making excuses of one sort or another of why we can't really make changes and to our ears this sound plausible but the real Truth is (if we develop HONESTY) that we don't really want to let go. We are really quite happy and contend to remain the old self and although there are wistful moments when we wished we could reach out in aspiration, we allow these holds to remain around us and put out all kinds of excuses to cover ourselves.

Fear is the root of all our problems and we allow this fear to rule us because we are afraid to search for Truth, and so we therefore remain in ignorance. To search for Truth, we must be prepared to sacrifice all those perceptions that we have held dear and that is familiar to us and the most painful part is the realization that only we can do this for ourselves. We need to understand that our so-called emotions is not usually real love. Real love does not bind nor does it give you pain. Real love is unconditional.

We need to understand that in this search the quickest and surest path is to go within. But this road to the highest, this search for truth, need not be done alone, nor in sorrow, for although we must search for our own individual truth, we are helped by our group soul who are undergoing the experiences with you, who share the load as you travel wearily on this path. They will help and guide you in your soul's search. No man is an island and yet each man must be his own saviour. What we achieve as individuals will light the way for others to follow.

Fear can be transmuted by Light. If we bathe ourselves in Light, if perhaps we may like to use an affirmation, we can gently and slowly eradicate fear. Maybe a useful affirmation to use is:

I AM LIGHT. MY LIGHT OVERCOMES ALL DARKNESS

PRIDE

Self-pride is the cloak that veils your vision. It is the armour that we put around us as a shield against Truth. Are we really aware of how much pride we have? Each time we hear something about ourselves that we dislike or feel unfair, a little prickly surge rises within us in either hurt or indignation. It's unfair, it's unjust, we say. If we knew ourselves truly well, if we faced truth then these little comments from others would have no effect on us because we would have reached that level of understanding that we would either accept it as a justifiable comment or we would understand that perhaps the other person made that comment from a space within themselves needing to learn a specific lesson.

But pride is a much wider and complicated subject. If we glanced at our lives we would recognise that pride is the root of judgment. We are constantly judging every condition and happening of our daily lives and we do this clouded by self-pride, family pride, and environmental conditioning, national pride and quite often we may not think of ourselves as proud people and believe ourselves to be fairly humble. But our vision is clouded because we do not recognise pride and perhaps mistake it for dignity or honour. There should be dignity and honour of the spirit but there is no place for any kind of pride if we wish to aspire to the highest.

Pride takes form in many different ways. Look around you, are you proud of what you have achieved; are you proud of your home; are you proud of your family; search every condition in your life and recognise pride – if anyone criticised any of these conditions would you be angry, upset, hurt or irritated? You may ask – what is wrong with being proud of our achievements, our families etc. The answer is – no, it isn't wrong to be happy about what we have achieved. It isn't wrong to feel that sense of accomplishment of something well done. However, there is a difference between the sense of joy of an achievement of a job well done or of a gift you have shared and the feeling that you have done something better than others. It all comes down to your reaction to that accomplishment, that gift. Do you understand the real meaning of PRIDE? Pride is an isolated emotion – it isolates you from your fellow-man. It separates you and what you have from others – it makes you feel different; it may even make you feel you are better than others. Pride may block us from giving true compassion, true understanding to others, because it isolates us. Pride is like cutting off the blood-line from you and your brother.

Pride may stop you from listening and learning because you may think you know more or better than your brother. We tend to accept teachings or only listen those whose appearance fit in with our orthodox upbringing and because of this we may miss opportunities to learn or hear words of value from someone else who may be of a different culture or race, because we are too proud to think that they could teach us something.

Our culture divides and categorises us into different classes – rich, middle class, working class, religion, caste etc. Pride rages through all these classes even amongst the poorest because pride veils itself in many varied forms. Snobbery is a form of pride but snobbery is not only the monopoly of the upper classes.

Are we too proud to admit to mistakes or errors? Do we feel we are lowering ourselves by doing this? If we are rejected, we feel the hurt but Pride is the one that hurts most and needs the gentle hand of love and compassion to overcome. Once we learn to be honest and love ourselves as we truly are; once we learn humility in all our actions and thoughts, then the veil of pride will fall from us, leaving the shining light standing naked in front of that mirror. Perhaps a useful affirmation:

I AM ONE WITH ALL LIFE

SPIRITUAL ARROGANCE

The realization that we could be accused of spiritual arrogance may come as a shock to those aspirants on the Path. We prefer to believe that we could not possibly be guilty of such a thing, for after all are we not on the path? But not so. The higher our aspirations, the greater the temptations and tests. If anything as we progress the tests get harder and more difficult to understand.

But spiritual arrogance is something that most aspirants fall prey to because the Path is so unique and the awakening awareness is such a wonder that it is so easy to think that we have discovered something rather special. This is all part of the process of the awakening consciousness and once we understand and go through this stage we then realise that on our own we are nothing but together we make up the Whole. And yet we have to seek and find the one true source within ourselves, to be complete.

We cannot go forward on the Path if we forget that our fellow travellers are travelling the same road and need a helping hand. Arrogance isolates us, we put blinkers on and fail to see the hurt we may be causing by our isolation. We should be prepared to share the knowledge we have acquired and the experiences we have gone through, for in sharing not only is the load halved but we can learn so much more.

Spiritual arrogance is the worst kind of sin because we are using spiritual knowledge to look down on our brother. We are so puffed up in our own discovery and self-importance that we get caught up in an illusory idea that that knowledge or experience is unique to us and by that virtue makes us somewhat "different" or "better" than others. The irony of this is that often we are not even aware of this "arrogance" and if anyone should accuse us of this, we are hurt and upset and indignant by this accusation. We prefer to think of ourselves as being so spiritual that we could not possibly be guilty of this dreadful "arrogance".

It is only when we face Truth in that mirror that we can recognise it and this realisation usually comes as a great shock. It is so easy not to see our greater weaknesses and the greater the weakness, the greater the shock. When we lift our heads again and look into that mirror squarely, we see ourselves differently, not as the outer physical eyes would like to see us, but as we truly are.

As we continue the path and we start stripping off the layers that bind us, we will notice a different "us" emerging. That new person may be a little unfamiliar, a little uncertain, but at least it's a more honest person. Gradually we get to know this person better and as the confidence builds up we will find an inner surge of strength and fortitude to carry on even more strongly in the search. This inner person is the real us, the beautiful light that has been hidden behind the scars; the jewel that has been polished by all the experiences of our struggles and battles. The rose that has been waiting to blossom by all the fruits of our endeavours, the one true being at-one with the Universe. And so we learn to trust. Affirmation:

I REJOICE IN MY UNITY WITH ALL LIFE

COURAGE

Courage comes from the inner strength that has built up through our many experiences and lessons. This is not a courage of the physical body but a courage that is built on a steady, reliable and constant knowing of who we are. Once acquired it cannot be lost for, like the spark of light within, this courage is of the spirit and cannot be extinguished.

To unfold this courage we need to be focussed on the inner light. There are and will be many tests that will challenge this courage in different ways. All those walking on the Path will be faced with tremendous opportunities to become aware of this courage which is inherent within. This is the courage that is needed when you are faced with derision about your beliefs or values. When faced with this onslaught, it is so easy to succumb and become one of the crowd who prefers to walk in ignorance and darkness. The temptations of belonging, the fear of being rejected and ridiculed are all part of the tests of the courage of the spirit.

But if we are strong in our convictions and beliefs, which comes from that inner knowledge, then we must be ready and prepared to face these tests squarely and with calmness in our hearts. If necessary we must be prepared to find ourselves alone, rejected even by loved ones. If you have set yourself on the path, if you have made the expansion and growth of your soul a target, then you must be prepared to face all these and allow that light, that inner strength, to guide you over the obstacles that will surely come your way.

There are many types of courage. There are those who are called upon to endure physical suffering; those who are mentally being exposed to derision and ridicule; those who are emotionally rejected and hurt. Many tears may be shed and many a bitter pill to swallow. If you stand up to fight for the right and freedom of spirit, you are throwing down a gauntlet to others. This is a challenge to the ignorant and the weak and their way of fighting back is to get at you and destroy you, for you are making them face themselves and this they cannot bear to do. So many are afraid of facing the Mirror of Truth. And if you, by your speech and actions, show them that Mirror, you will find yourself a target for their onslaught based on fear and ignorance.

At these times your only refuge is that inner contact, that inner light that remains as a rock within, steadfast and reliable. It can never be extinguished. This will be your source to remain true and constant. This will be your shield, your armour against the barrage of abuse and rejection. You need never fear of being alone or unloved for when you have found the light within, it will supply all your needs of courage, strength and love. Affirmation:

I AM STRENGTH, I STAND UP FOR MY TRUTH

DISCRIMINATION

Discrimination between what is perceived as right and wrong; between the outer and inner self, the personality and the soul, positive and negative, truth and ignorance. This is such an important quality on the spiritual path. Almost every decision we make is based on the correct application of discrimination.

What is discrimination? Is it just a question of choosing between right and wrong? It is for each of us to examine what we basing our decisions upon. What is the importance of discrimination? Why is discrimination the key of sounding the right note?

In the first instance we are usually brought up to know the difference between good and evil, right or wrong, black and white. This is part of our upbringing and we accept this as part of society's rules. It is a form of conditioning for these concepts have been derived at by centuries of man-made laws and orthodox teachings – it is also judgmental. But when we set ourselves upon the path we discover that there are far more aspects of discrimination than we realised.

One of the first hurdles on the journey of discovery is the discovery itself of how many different paths there are. Although all paths lead to the one true source, one needs to find out which path is the right one for us at this stage of our evolution. And therefore the first confusion and doubts creep in. How does one choose this, how does one discriminate between the paths to find the right one?

The problem here is in discriminating the path that our personality (our lower self) would prefer to choose and that which our soul (our higher self) knows is the right one. So here therefore come the first lesson in discrimination. When on the spiritual path (and remember that not all on the spiritual path are conscious of this) it is so easy to think that since your motives are altruistic that they must therefore be correct. One of the hardest lesson is to realise that what you would like to do (no matter how pure the motives) is not necessarily what your spirit, your soul wants you to do. And so you need to learn how to tell the difference, to discriminate between the path of your soul and the path your personality would like you to take. How does one do this? How can one possibly tell the difference? Which path do you take? Which teachings do you follow?

There are indeed many questions such as these that you could ask yourself. There are many avenues that you could search which may either help or confuse you more. The answers lie, not on the outside, but on the inner level. Your soul will answer your calling if you remember to go within and let yourself be guided by that inner light which is the source of all knowledge, all wisdom. This will never fail you if you sound the right note. What is meant by the right note? Very simply, unselfish motives, surrender to the Divine Will, the highest within you, in other words the essence of spirit.

It is important to remember that the more balanced you are the easier it will be to discriminate. If you are swayed by your emotions like a pendulum, or your mind is too analytical and exacting, you will not be able to discern or discriminate from the true heart. One must always aim to be perfectly poised and balanced in the light so that our discrimination is based on our ability to stand back and observe with the eye of spirit, with a clear mind and a loving heart.

Perhaps the hardest example of this is when we need to make a decision concerning loved ones, for usually we tend to let our emotions cloud our judgment. We would find these decisions easier to arrive at if we could always remember to view life with the concept that we are spirit first and matter second and if we would allow that inner guidance to flow through us, prompting us to think and live according to spiritual law. Along with discrimination comes discernment. It is difficult to discern from the personality but much easier when we are following our inner in-tuition. Affirmation:

I AM THE CENTRE OF LIFE, I AM THE BALANCE. I CHOOSE TRUTH

HUMILITY

Perhaps of all the qualities on the path, this is the one that truly opens us more to the Christ-like gentleness. The more we learn, the greater the tests and lessons, the more humble we become, because we realise how small we are in comparison with the greatness and glory of the Absolute.

Humility comes from a simple loving heart which has accepted and surrendered the Will of the Personality to the highest. The heart which has seen the glory of the Absolute manifested in every aspect of life. To be humble does not mean to cower under stronger forces. It does not mean that you should take everything that life throws at you with a resigning will. To be humble means that you recognise the Divine Will and act on it, and that all your successes and achievements all belong to the glory of the Divine Spirit within, because that light within you is guiding your efforts and your endeavours and what you achieve is done through the divine will, the essence of spirit within. When you fight the good fight all the forces of righteousness are thrown in behind you. Humility is the realization that man on his own is nothing and it is only the guiding light within, the spark of the Absolute within each that is responsible for all achievements. It is the spirit within that is the guiding force of all our achievements, all our attainments.

Humility is realising that your fellow-man is also undergoing great tests and trials and that his path is just as difficult as yours and that therefore you should never judge his motives or his actions for he too has that spark of the Divine within.

Humility is facing up to yourself honestly. We are strengthened by the courage that we have attained, by the truth of our very being. The mirror of Truth can teach us so much but we must look at ourselves holistically and not as a small part with imperfections. As a whole we understand and realise the beauty of creation and in this realisation we are humbled by the wonders and magnificence of spirit.

Let us always remember that we, as human beings, are not the only ones of the Absolute Being's creation. Let us widen our knowledge and open our eyes to the whole of creation, to the other kingdoms in nature, to the rest of the universe of which we know so little and yet we are all inter-related. Look to the skies above, look to the earth around you, see this creation see this wonder and when we can take in this infinitesimal percentage of this work, we will know and understand true humility. The humility of knowing that of ourselves we are nothing, that without this life, this essence, within us, we would not even exist.

Let us also humbly remember that we never work alone. We are part of a group of family. That each of us contribute a quality, a piece of a jig-saw, which is necessary to the other. Sometimes our proud physical mind may credit ourselves with achievements of our own making, but this is not so. We are surrounded by helpers' unseen to assist us along the path. These are aspects of our group soul willing us on with inspiration and guidance. With their love they give us courage and strength to keep on keeping on when the going gets rough.

By our own individual experiences we help each other. If we sound the right note within our heart there is always someone there to help us. We are part of each other. Part of the Whole. And it is this realization that brings us humility. We work as a group, as a family, for the good of humanity, because as we progress individually and collectively, so does humanity progress to. This is spiritual law – one cannot advance without the other. As we go forward we take the whole of humanity with us. Affirmation:

I REJOICE IN MY BEINGNESS WITH ALL LIFE

DETACHMENT

One of the greatest stumbling block along the spiritual path is attachment. We attach ourselves to relationships, conditions, circumstances, places, situations etc. Our emotions and our thoughts are so caught up in all these that it is so very difficult to be objective in our reasoning, in our reactions. There is a great need for the aspirant to start working on balancing emotions and thoughts. We do this by understanding that our emotions and our thoughts are not the whole of us. There is the soul, the spirit which guides us through life after life. Look at it like a see-saw, put the emotions on one side and the thoughts on another. See yourself, your real self, in the centre, balancing these two. Life often throws at us a barrage of problems, issues to resolve. We are often faced with emotional trauma, not always our own but family or friends, and it is very difficult to deal with this when we are caught up in the middle. We truly cannot be objective nor indeed helpful to others if we respond to the problem through our emotions or through our perception.

Therefore, the quality of detachment is one that we need to work upon and manifest in our lives to help us respond to life's issues in a calm, and positive manner. We can also be of much more use to family and friends from this detached position. We need to remember that detachment does not mean being cold and unfeeling. It means looking at a situation with clarity, allowing our inner wisdom to manifest and discern between the emotions surrounding the problem and the reality.

It is also worth noting that we can become attached to organisations, societies because we may find a common belief. This is good and for a period of time it may be just what we need. But do remember that we are ever growing, ever unfolding and the time may come when that particular organisation or society no longer feeds your spiritual needs. This then is the time to become detached and move on. Always grateful for the experiences, for the lessons and for the teachings that have come your way which will always stay an intrinsic part of you. Affirmation:

I REMAIN TRUE TO MY INNER SELF

EXPANDING THE VISION

It is so easy and natural when one is in a physical body to assume that what is around us is all there is. Even when one is on a spiritual path we relate our lives to our own environment i.e. our family, our work, our community and our country. We try to put into action by our thoughts, words or deeds the knowledge that we have achieved by our aspirations and efforts. Many of us also relate in different ways to the natural and animal kingdom around us. We need to, however, expand our vision further and recognise what a vast ocean of knowledge and living there is still untapped with us.

By limiting our vision to ourselves and our immediate outer surroundings we remain in ignorance of our true self, our true potential, and because of this we hold back the expansion and progress of the earth planet and humanity. If each of us became aware of our true self, if we explored this vast ocean within us, we would be like pioneers venturing forth into the unknown, armed just with courage and a dream of something better and wonderful waiting for us. What we may discover may not be quite what we expected but we would be the richer for that knowledge and experience and would have opened a gateway for others to follow.

Within us is unlimited resources of wealth of knowledge, of wisdom, of strength and courage and with this expansion comes greater depths of love bringing us much deeper understanding, patience and tolerance of all our problems and especially of our fellow-men.

When we set forth on the journey of self-discovery we were given a parcel, a ruck-sack, containing all the qualities that we have unfolded over many lifetimes necessary to assist us as we make our way through the experiences of the earthly planet. Nothing is forgotten. All we need and have ever needed is in that parcel within us for us to call upon. But we have blinded ourselves and put a chain around that parcel and forgotten about it. We have been caught up in the miasma and glamour of the earthly life.

The only requisite needed to open that parcel is true aspiration to do good, to fulfil our purpose as individual souls. If our motives are pure then that chain will fall away and the veil will be lifted and the qualities needed will rise to the surface to go through our experiences. We must learn to put aside the outer egoic impulses that send us hither and dither. We need to become centralised and focus our whole being in our heart centre concentrating purely on finding that balance between heart and mind – true heart and mind.

We need to be so centred that no emotions will sway us, no mental argument or conflict disturb us nor a cold intellect separate our vision from the heart, no matter how logical the reasoning may be. When we learn how to become centred then our decisions will be taken away from the outer mind. Instead we will act, think and speak from the true source of our being. It will be the higher intuition which will guide all our endeavours, no matter where it may lead and because we have allowed the true Christ Being, the Cosmic Light, within us to guide us, we will be impervious to any form of unkind or unjust action against us. Our true self will understand the deeper meaning behind every condition of life, thus uplifting and carrying us forward through every experience and condition.

No longer will we be perturbed by any experience that comes our way for we will understand and recognise all happenings as part of the great plan, the great unfoldment necessary for our development and progress as an individual soul, as part of a group soul and as part of the whole concept of evolution. This may sound so far-fetched and incredulous as to be beyond the normal person in this lifetime; but not so, each one can experience this is we truly and honestly set out to find ourselves.

Everything that happens to us, every detail of our daily lives has a fundamental meaning, it portrays an outward expression of an inner condition and we can gain so much knowledge of ourselves and surroundings if we observe our daily happenings and try and find an inner reason. By this observation we can determine what lessons we are undergoing, whether we are learning them or whether we need further opportunities for that lesson to be properly learned. We therefore expand our vision of ourselves and of the conditions around us.

Above all, we are not limiting ourselves by putting blockages and saying 'we are what we are and we can't change in this lifetime'. That is not so We can change ourselves if we wanted to. We all have the potential qualities within us to do this – it's all in that parcel. What we need to do is to ask ourselves – do we want to look at the mirror and see ourselves as we are. Do we want to be honest and face truths about ourselves? Isn't it always much easier to blame others for our problems? Isn't it easier to just ignore and carry on as normal?

There are questions which each one of us can ask ourselves. How much do we want to learn about ourselves and the purpose of our incarnation? How much do we want to dig deep down? We don't have to; we don't need to. We can just amble along through life as best we can and wait until we are over the veil to find out more about this. But there will come a time, a moment whether in this lifetime or in another, when the soul will reach a stage when it needs to know more; it will no longer be satisfied with ambling along; it wants to get hold of its destiny face it and see where it's going, what it has achieved, what other lessons are needed. And then the soul, of its own volition, will become the captain of its ship, it will guide its own destiny, it will face the turbulent seas and storms and steer it through to calmer waters. It will know what is in that parcel and will call upon each quality as it is needed for each different experience, each different lesson. It will become Master of its Path.

As we grow in understanding, as we begin to see the outworking of Divine Law, we realise that all our fretting and worrying about this and that was so unnecessary. If we could learn to be still and let our inner self guide our path, we would save ourselves so much stress and anxiety. It does work if we are patient enough to let it happen, if we trust and have faith and confidence in the Divine Will which guides us. And because we allow that inner light to flow naturally, things work out as they should work out, without any stress or problems.

By allowing this inner light to guide our life we are then able to see conditions around us more clearly and thus our vision is expanded by our clearer understanding of events and reactions by others. A clearer vision, not only helps us in our own circumstances but also by allowing that pure light to flow, we permeate this light in any and every surrounding we find ourselves in, thus healing and enlightening as we do so. We are then raising our own consciousness above the earthly turmoil and that of others for it follows a pattern of natural and spiritual law.

We have the choices right here and now in our physical consciousness to decide which way we want to go – the easy or the hard way. We will consciously be in command. Our inner light is truly Master of all our Being.

As we expand our inner vision we begin to relate to our environment, our family, our community, our nation and to the earth planet with a different degree of consciousness. We begin to understand the happenings of world affairs and conflicts, the reasoning and working out of the Divine plan. Our understanding will change as our degree of consciousness changes. We may find ourselves more drawn to other nations, especially those whose people are in great need, and this may be because of a past link and therefore we are in a position now to possibly help that nation and its people by either physical, financial help or by our prayers.

We begin to see our place in the pattern of life on this planet and we grow in deeper understanding when such things as disasters or famines occur. We learn to respond freely to people from different parts of the world because we understand that this is a brother or sister undergoing their own experiences, learning similar lessons but in different circumstances, a different nation maybe and even a different race. By this understanding and clarity, we truly become co-creators with the Divine Will.

To be a co-creator with the Divine Will means that we are no longer willing to stand back and wait for 'something' or 'someone' to tell us what to do or guide us forward. To be a co-creator means we take hold of our destiny, we understand the qualities necessary to unfold for our continued growth and we put ourselves in the circumstances or situations necessary for this growth. We accept our Path, our Destiny and our place in the greater scheme of life.

By expanding our vision, we will know the meaning of at-one-ment with the Universal Life and all its Creation.

CHAPTER 8

Karma & Past Lives

What is Karma?

Karma is simply an opportunity to learn. The expression as we sow, so we reap, is a very true one but the reaping of karma is not evil nor vindictive. It is simply an opportunity of learning the lessons we have not learned previously. Remember that the soul chooses before its incarnation, through the benefit of looking at the Akashic records, what experiences it needs to continue its growth and development. If the soul realises that in past lives it didn't learn a lesson well, perhaps because of undeveloped soul qualities, or for other reasons, then it may choose to come back to ensure that initial lesson is well and truly learned. The soul comes back with a blue-print of what it would like to learn in any lifetime. The actual circumstances and details may not be clear nor known. The soul takes the journey and although at an inner level it has chosen its parents and environment, the details of that journey are more or less indeterminate as so many other factors, such as family circumstances, culture and national karma are involved.

What can we learn from past lives?

In every life, we accumulate karma. Karma is a result of our thoughts, deeds and actions. Therefore, it follows that good thoughts, deeds and actions will accrue good karma – in other words look at it like amassing credits for the soul. Equally, unkind, destructive thoughts, deeds and actions will accrue the opposite, debits – as we sow, so shall we reap! Karma is the most wonderful opportunity the soul has to truly progress and evolve along the path. There is no such thing as bad karma. It can only be described as bad by those who do not understand Karma and furthermore if we are negative about life and we see all experiences as mishaps, then we have yet to learn the clarity of spiritual understanding. I do not apologise for repeating, again and again, karma is a wonderful opportunity to learn.

Whatever experiences the soul has undergone in past lives will have resulted in accruing some kind of karma. Sometimes karma may result in your needing to deal with unjust criticism – perhaps you were judgmental of another in a past life. There are many examples and reasons. However, in this life you may have the opportunity to face that karma and transmute it. How can we transmute this? How can we change what may have happened in the past of which we have no knowledge of in this life? Very simply, deal with whatever circumstance you are faced with by right thinking, right feeling, right action. It is always wise to pause for a moment before reacting to a situation, however difficult this may be. By pausing, we allow our inner wisdom, our inner light to guide us to react from a true heart. Often, we allow our emotions and our thoughts to overrule us and then it is like being tossed in a storm, totally out of control. Instead allow the captain of our ship to guide us through the stormy seas. In other words, allow your true self, your soul, your spirit to lead you forward. When this happens, you respond, you react in such a way that the other person does not feel threatened. You have mastered a situation and transmuted karma instead of adding further karma.

In my Talks and Workshops, I give out an exercise to use which might be helpful. That is:

- Train yourself to 'pause for a moment' each time you are faced with a situation, perhaps unkind words from another. That pause – even for a couple of seconds – will be enough to allow your soul to respond. Therefore, you are not reacting from emotions or thoughts, but rather you are responding from the soul. Often you will find that when you do this you have deflated a situation and rather than an angry reaction going backwards and forwards like a ping-pong game, your calmer response will also calm the situation around you. Try it, it really works!

The Karma of Nations, including Group Karma

We need to understand that as there is karma for individual souls, there is also karma for groups and nations. The earth itself is a living soul and therefore all living things, accumulate karma over aeons of years. Those who live and breathe on earth are responsible for the evolution of earth. Deeds that have transgressed natural law will need to be accounted for by the Lords of Karma. As we sow, we reap!

Is Karma a punishment?

Sadly, many see karma as some form of punishment and that some horrible fate may befall us through karma. This is not so. Look at karma as a wonderful teacher who helps you to understand lessons. This teacher may have to at times rebuke you for not paying attention, for not being responsible for your thoughts, deeds or actions. But this teacher is understanding, only puts you through the lessons it knows you can cope with. This teacher knows what soul qualities you have unfolded and developed that will help you go through that condition or experience. At an inner level, you yourself have chosen which karma to transmute in any one lifetime. When you are faced with a harsh situation, a difficult relationship, with lack in your life, try to understand why this may be happening. Turn your thoughts inwards and look in that mirror. Why have you brought this experience to yourself? What do you need to learn from this? How can you deal with this? How can you overcome and rise above it? What is it teaching me?

What does it really mean?

All this means is that your soul is simply going through the stepping stones of your journey. Each lifetime, each experience is a learning process, slowly unfolding, slowly developing. Building that antahkarana, this means the bridge reaching ever forward and upwards to recognise your own spirituality.

When we can recognise and accept this, it makes the journey easier. It is like going up the mountain, perilous though it may have been at times, suddenly you find yourself almost there. Not so far to go now. Perhaps time for a rest, make use of all those credits we have amassed, have an easier life, until we catch our breath and be ready to move on up towards the mountain-top.

Let us look at Karma without fear and welcome it as a friend and teacher who is here to help us learn. Once we can accept that karma is inevitable, we may even find that it is not so bad after all! The only thing that we fear is simply our perception of Karma. Get rid of that perception. Allow the veil to be torn apart and as you shine in your Light, your true vestment, you will rejoice at the wonderful opportunities that will come your way and how they are taking you forward along each stepping stone on your journey of self-discovery.

CHAPTER 9

Deeper Knowledge of the Spiritual Path

The spiritual path has many expressions or perhaps I should say representations. It very much depends on us which expression or representation appeals to us and what may give us a deeper understanding of this incredible and wondrous subject. Some are simpler than others. The following may give you an inkling of the ones which have helped me particularly along the way. There are many others of course but it is up to everyone to seek knowledge in whichever direction it feels drawn to. Remember though, that there are also many pitfalls along the path. Use discrimination, discernment and truth constantly and wisely.

What are Symbols?

Symbols were a form of teaching used by the Ancients to teach and inspire, to identify with specific causes. Most of our primal symbols come from a time prior to verbal communication as we know it today and most certainly predate the written word, which itself obliterates much of the need for pictorial symbols. Apart from the very modern signs, which are more or less common knowledge as to their meaning, for the most part these pictorial metaphors must remain open to speculation and intuition.

Symbols are not static objects as their interpretation and meaning continue to develop. It is worthwhile looking at ancient symbols, observing it and heed its message. Symbols were used to identify with a particular idea. They were symbolic of ideals and most importantly of bringing to the people the understanding of the universal order in a simplistic form. They were given to instruct the masses of Ideals, Identification, Religious interpretation, spiritual understanding.

In the olden days, banners were used in battle to identify with kings and leaders. Ones that are easy to recognise today are The Lions of Scotland; The Dragon of Wales and The St. George Cross of England.

Interestingly enough, the Eagle has been the symbol for different empires, the Egyptian, the Romans and now the symbol for the US.

Nowadays we have logos – it is how we identify a particular company, corporations with a specific item.

Other symbols that we may recognise and which has been used throughout history which has been used by the authorities or religion are the Orb; the Rod of Power; the Tudor Rose; the Crescent Banner; the Zodiac signs and not forgetting the flag of the Pirates which had a skeleton as identification.

But there are major symbols which are very ancient and are very symbolic. Some we may understand, others we won't but nevertheless they play an intrinsic part in our creation. These are:

The dot is the very beginning of creation; a beginning and a conclusion. A seed full of potential and a symbol of the Supreme and Absolute Being.

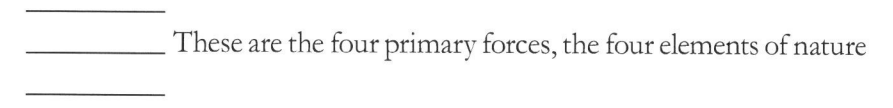

_____

_____ These are the four primary forces, the four elements of nature

_____

- o The Circle is the symbol of the Deity – the ONE. The circle has no beginning, no end. It is the Alpha and Omega. It symbolises infinity, everlasting, without end. It is also space – think of the concept of zero. Think of the realisation that 'nothing' can be 'something'. Without this space, there is no area for anything to exist. Think of a blank page – if you wished to write or draw, you need a page, on a blank page you can create anything you wish. This absence of any thing means that 'no thing' is the most important symbol in the world.

⊙ Perhaps the one symbol that is consistent throughout is the DOT within the circle. This represents the beginnings of Earth within the circle of Divinity. In other words, it could be interpreted as man having free will and is protected within the circle of the Divine.

+ Another important symbol is the equal-sided cross. The cross is a very ancient symbol. It symbolises humanity. The cross brings us the balance of life. It represents the equal balance between the spirit, the physical, the emotions and the mental bodies. The cross is the very heart of life on earth. We need to be truly balanced in all our subtler bodies. It symbolises the four elements of nature; the four major initiations.

⊕ Then we have the cross within the circle. This symbolises man, within the Universe, the Deity. The four elements, the four forces symbolised by the Cross. With the Circle drawn around the Cross it symbolises the ancient's Divinity of Five, i.e. the Deity and His Four Great Primary Forces, the four elements, Earth, Air, Fire, Water. These ancient symbols were used in Temples of old to teach people the way of life and initiating those who are ready into the mysteries of creation.

□ As the Deity was represented by the Circle so the Square represents Earth. This is the symbol of Earth. Its purpose was also to teach primitive man the four points North, South, East and West. It also represents the Four Great Primary Forces, joined together. These forces first evolved law and order out of chaos and darkness. It is also the roots, the very foundation of the Pyramid.

Δ The foundation of the Pyramid is the square. Raised from the roots, the square, the Pyramid is the aspiration to the highest. We reach up to the Divine. The equal-sided triangle forms the triune Godhead. One in three – three in One. It is a usual fact of nature that we always aspire upwards.

★ The six-pointed Star is the symbol of the new Age. Its upward pointing triangle symbolises humanity aspiring upwards towards the highest. The downward pointing triangle is the Highest, the Godhead reaching down towards humanity.

Synchronicity

Very often in life things happen to us which are not always easy to define. At different times in our lives we ask for help for different reasons but the answers don't necessarily come as we expect them. However, do remember that our prayers, our plea for help is always heard. Our soul, our spirit will respond. How this response appears depends very much on how receptive we are. Sometimes we may get the answer through someone else's lips as they talk to us; sometimes we are drawn to read a book and words seem to jump at us. Sometimes a thought pops into our brain. If for whatever reason we do not heed the first response, then spirit will find a way to ensure that this is repeated maybe through another form. This is called synchronicity. When something comes to you from different directions – be open, take heed, your question has been heard.

Sometimes life has a way of bringing things together from different sources and you may wonder 'Wow, how did that happen? 'Simple, that is synchronicity! Don't dismiss it. Follow it.

What is a Mystic?

A mystic sees the greater and deeper purpose behind life and all happenings. There are three stages of a mystic:

- Awakening – Searching – at soul level – Dissatisfaction with the ordinary life

    By feeling dissatisfied with answers, with things around us. Our search starts. We know there is more. We start becoming detached from familiar reasoning, happenings. We question more. Why? Does it make sense? This is a soul quest. At soul level, we question all that has satisfied us thus far.

- Finding – Awareness – Searching and finding who we are

    We come across a new way of thinking – does our heart respond? We hear something new that sends a tingle down our spine? Are we connecting with a new awareness? At some level, we are responding but we are not completely sure what this is yet? But if we are open to new or different Teaching then we are connecting at soul level.

- Sharing – Living our Truth – when we reach this realisation – let us Walk our Talk

    We can become quite excited by a new awareness that has come to us. This comes from an inner realisation that we have found something very special. Let's share this. Let's put this new awareness, this finding into practice. Let's walk our Talk.

How do we bring mysticism into a living reality?

- By being aware constantly of the inner you – the I AM – remembering who we are, where we came from – let us first embrace who we are and then let us embody who we are. Let it become a way of life. It is taking us from within to without.
- By being, by living, by enjoying being in the world – ultimate detachment. This means living in a state of grace, thankfulness, forgiveness, awareness.
- By always remembering & maintaining that link with the greater picture/inner purpose. By recognising the deeper mystery that dwells within us and around us.
- By acknowledging the human need/personality.
- By not judging yourself/others – i.e. not beating yourself up.

- By considering how many other belief systems/indoctrination can be determining your human perception.
- By developing sensitivity & tolerance to others' feelings
- By listening to all sides but remaining unaffected by politics, religion, current affairs.
- By showing detachment
- By allowing for changes i.e. new thoughts, perceptions to materialise
- By giving your soul time for lessons to be learned at all levels.
- To bring sacred balance to all that is.
- To remember our spiritual qualities and bring these into manifestation through our life and work in the world
- To reconnect with those who came before us and those who will come after us.
- To remember that we are co-creators of this world and it is our responsibility to create a better future for our children.
- Have our experiences, our meditations, transported us into a different level of awareness?
- How can we bring this into our daily lives? How can we negotiate these moments of bliss, of joy, and live them in the practical world?

What is a practical mystic?

A practical mystic can touch into their mystical and true self while living in everyday life and its challenges. In this realisation of awareness, you can experience the power and joy of your personal freedom. When this happens you automatically wish to share this with all those you interact with. A practical mystic lives out that purpose in daily life. In ancient days, one could say that the practical mystics were the shamans, the medicine men and women, those who mediated and interacted with the unseen worlds to bring knowledge, balance, healing, ceremony, art, peace, prophecy and abundance to their people. This knowledge and gift were shared with all the other forms of life amongst whom they lived in sacred relationship.

We need to learn to live in this state of awareness and if necessary we need to withdraw our energy, our perception, our desires from the old choices, the old perceptions of ourselves which has held us imprisoned and be more allied with that which makes us more whole, more aware of the mystical aspect of life in our everyday life.

Are we willing to do this? Everything we do, think and feel is energy. We can change energy.

It serves here to remind ourselves how energy, perceptions, feelings can control us. If we think negatively or pessimistically; if we resist any emotions or thoughts which challenge us. When we resist, it has the opposite effect and in fact it persists. By resisting we are in fact separating ourselves from true feelings and this detracts us from living in unity with life.

So, what can we do to help ourselves? It becomes easier when we start seeing the difference between the emotions, the mind and the soul. Remember the cross of life. The equal-sided cross, with the spiritual at the top, the physical at the bottom and the emotions and mind on either side. It is about finding that balance. It is about finding that centre and living from that centre which is all light and love. When we can start doing this, any false perceptions or beliefs fall away and this releases any deep-seated fears. Clarity will come and we will find unity in that balance, in that new awareness.

What are Initiations?

Initiation means quite simply an expansion of consciousness. During the course of many lives we go through a series of initiations which will finally free us from the continuous round of earthly incarnations. There are three major initiations related to the physical plane, the soul plane and the spiritual. But there are also four other very important initiations related to the four elements, i.e. Water, Air, Fire and Earth. Furthermore, there are also minor ones which in their turn relate to the different aspects of our Being.

Every experience we go through, from the least to the most profound, forms a part of one or other of these major initiations by which we eventually gain mastery over ourselves, mastery over the circumstances of our lives, and mastery over the very substance of matter itself.

We prepare and experience different degrees of initiations at the same time, although we may not have completed any one of them.

Throughout the history of humanity, there have been examples of a life which has exemplified the life of every soul. One of these was of course the life of the Master Jesus. His life demonstrated the path of every soul and indeed the initiations he went through, culminating in the great initiation of the crucifixion and resurrection, the 4th Initiation.

First, we need to understand what an initiation is. We do this by considering what the journey of the soul is and what exactly is the nature of its incarnation.

When a soul comes down into incarnation, it has to go through the experiences of three of its layers. These are the subtler bodies which we know as the mental, emotional and physical. This makes up our personality.

Most people are only familiar with the personality as the presence of the soul may not yet be understood. As has been mentioned before, the purpose of our lives is for the soul to manifest itself and take control, to master the three subtler bodies of emotions, mind and physical. So these three also referred to as three of the elements of nature, i.e. Water, Air, Earth are related to the first three initiations.

Initiations are something that takes place at soul level, not at the physical. It is experienced by the soul at its own level. Each initiation means that the soul has gained mastery over one of the subtler bodies, i.e. one of the elements of nature. Initiations are taken over many lifetimes and are truly a slow process. Initiations are a valuable and essential phase of our spiritual evolution. Each initiation marks an achievement; it indicates that the soul has attained greater direction over the personality through which it is trying to express itself.

Initiation as well as being a mark of achievement is also an opportunity for new beginnings as the soul then is ready for a new level of consciousness.

When the soul has undergone an Initiation, it is aware of a deeper responsibility and it heightens the will to serve through the process of growth along the path.

As we have said above, there are four major initiations related to the subtler bodies of the personality, these are:

WATER - Emotions (overcoming negative emotions which threaten to overwhelm us)
AIR - Mind (discerning between the outer mind which needs to control you, and the higher mind which brings you the wisdom of the soul)
FIRE - Love (understanding the difference between sentimentality, mawkishness and the true feelings of the heart)
EARTH - Living those lessons learned through the first three initiations and bringing those realities back to earth and living it. In other words, living our Truth.

What are the Elements?

The elements of nature are as mentioned above. The soul needs to balance the emotional body, the mental body, the spiritual and the physical. Again, I refer to the equal sided cross **+** perfectly balanced. We master the four elements of our nature and we stride forward as bearers of the Light.

What is Gnosis?

True Gnosis is the knowledge of the heart. Gnosis is the knowledge of ourselves. Humans are generally ignorant of the divine spark, the divine seed which is within them. This ignorance has been cultivated by the indoctrination and influence of those in positions of power who wished to keep people in ignorance, so that the people remain unaware of their true nature and destiny.

Gnosis is the knowledge we acquire through our own experiences, as opposed to knowledge that we are told or believe in. Gnosis is conscious, experiential knowledge, not merely intellectual or conceptual knowledge, belief, or theory. From Gnosis came the many philosophies, the sciences, the arts and the religions that have traditionally been prevalent on earth for so many hundreds of years. In the course of history, humans have progressed from the slavery of materialism, the gaining of spiritual freedom through the freedom of Gnosis. To understand Gnosis, we need to free ourselves from the ignorance that has besotted humanity for so long. The ignorance of spiritual realities is dispelled only by Gnosis and there have been wonderful teachers, messengers of light, light workers, who over the years have brought us revelation of Gnosis. One of these was the Master Jesus. It was by his teachings and his establishing of the ancient mysteries that Jesus performed his work of salvation and not only by his crucifixion.

Freedom and Salvation is brought about only by gnosis.

Gnosticism embraces the knowledge that we gain from our attitudes, our reactions towards life; it encourages non-attachment and non-conformity to the world, a 'being in the world, but not of the world'; a lack of egotism; and a respect for the freedom and dignity of other beings.

When Confucius was asked about death, he replied: 'Why do you ask me about death when you do not know how to live?' It is worthwhile remembering that death does not automatically bring about liberation from bondage unless one has lived one's life in the understanding of gnosis and by living it – in other words walking our talk, bringing spirituality down into matter and living it. In due course, and by following the spiritual path, every spiritual being will receive Gnosis and will be reunited with its higher Self but not without the sincere, honest and determined struggle for gnosis.

So how do we come to gnosis?

It is not something we can learn from a book or by listening to spiritual teachers.

It is not something we can pick up from therapy, nor regular meditation, although this helps to bring us to a quiet place within.

Gnosis can only come when we have experienced that inner realisation of a Truth.

When that happens we 'know' – we can say 'Now I understand' – 'now I know'.

This comes to us little by little - knowledge doesn't hit us like a tsunami. It comes gradually as we unfold our spirituality.

How to recognise 'knowledge'

Freedom and salvation comes about when we reach gnosis. What does this mean?

It means that we will reach a certain stage in our development when the material world of mind and emotions will no longer imprison us. We will be free of perceptions and indoctrination.

It means that our thoughts and emotions will no longer be our guiding force in everyday life but rather instruments available to us to teach us more about our reactions and where upon the stage of unfoldment we are. It takes time and many experiences to bring us to this realisation. It is our own truth that will be our salvation, that will gain us our freedom from materialistic slavery.

What do we mean by the 'stage of unfoldment & development'?

It is about realising how we have unfolded our spiritual qualities. What are these?

Our lessons are learned by the soul's reaction to the tests – not the tests themselves.

KNOW THYSELF AND THOU SHALT KNOW THE UNIVERSE

These ancient words were above the Temples of old. It is said that there is no condition or circumstance of life in which it would be impossible for any man or woman to serve as a son/daughter of Divine. As we travel the path, little by little, we have the opportunity to unfold and grow. As we grow we understand that developing ourselves, understanding who we really are will give us that greater and deeper understanding of creation. It is said that the universe is portrayed in our hands.

HOW DO WE KNOW OURSELVES?
By understanding our soul lessons – reminder of the Labours of Hercules.

Every experience, from the lesser to the greater, has deep significance along the journey. Eventually through the twelve great labours, the twelve soul lessons i.e. going through the twelve signs of the zodiac, the soul will overcome and become master over the elements of his nature. Two of the essential qualities that each soul has to learn along the path is that of discernment and discrimination. These truths can only be recognised from within. All these lessons are valuable and we cannot skip any. This is natural law.

By recognising our soul qualities
Each sign will give the soul the opportunity to unfold spiritual qualities, be they mercy, compassion, tolerance, patience, strength, courage etc. We unfold soul qualities by degrees and also through the understanding on the effect that the subtler bodies such as the emotions and the mind have on the soul. How do we recognise whether we have unfolded or developed spiritual qualities?

By introspection
The subtler bodies will often sway us hither and dither until we learn to be master of our own ship. The Soul is in control and needs to balance the subtler bodies in order to attain that degree of peace and harmony and rise in spirit to its highest consciousness. It's so necessary here not to let fear overwhelm us; we really do need to remember that we have a seed of the Divine within. We need to acknowledge that seed. Let this be our guiding light. Let this be our strength; our power. The affirmations can be so very helpful and we can make up our own. One special affirmation that I have always found very helpful is to keep saying 'I AM'. This is a recognition of our Beingness; an

acknowledgement of something greater within and also a declaration of a truth within.

It is in the stillness of our own heart that we find our Truth. This Truth is the same today as it was yesterday. One vital help along the way is to allow the time for Silence. Silence is very powerful for it is a state of being. It is in the silence that we can find out Truth, our Voice. These Truths were known to ancient philosophers as they are known to Teachers of Wisdom today. In moments of great anguish or great bewilderment it is so helpful to find a moment of Silence. For it is in the silence that wisdom can speak to us.

By meditation

By going within, contemplating and allowing our inner heart to teach us whatever our soul is in need to learn. By acknowledging the presence of those beings who are our helpers, our guides. By allowing ourselves the time and space to be at one with the spirit within.

By healing ourselves

Self-healing comes about when we attain an inner truth about ourselves; when we grow in understanding of WHO and WHAT we are, when we reach an inner realization (and we can say *'Ah, yes now I understand'*) a healing process begins to take place so that slowly we unfold spiritually and heal our soul at that deeper level, beyond the physical. Slowly, the soul learns to overcome its turbulent emotions, to still the anxious mind, to live tranquilly, kindly, lovingly, and the physical body housing the soul should become, in due time, healthy and eventually perfect – this is the goal of every soul.

By engaging in life

All souls have freewill choice as to the direction it follows and have to learn through their journey the qualities of discernment and discrimination. These truths can only be discerned from within, from the innermost spirit within each one of us. When these truths have been discerned, we need to engage in life so that we can share our truths, share our knowledge and above all share our love and light. We need to remember that we are human as well as divine and that the whole purpose of our lives is to bring spirituality down into matter. We have to transform matter through our developed spiritual qualities.

By Walking our Talk

Walking our Talk is about who we are, what we truly believe in, having the courage and strength to be exactly who we are. It is about following our own standards and principles, with integrity, honesty and steadiness. It is about being responsible for ourselves and how we behave towards others. It is about being our Truth. Until we know who or what we are, we cannot walk our talk. It will always be someone else's talk.

Socrates declared knowledge, virtue and utility to be one with the innate nature of good. Knowledge is a condition of knowing; virtue a condition of being; utility a condition of doing.

CHAPTER 10

Where do we go from here?

How does the knowledge of the spiritual world help us with the pressures of living?

In this modern society of ours we are always surrounded by pressures of one sort or another. And it is the way that we deal with these pressures that helps us to learn lessons. Sometimes these pressures may seem never-ending but sooner or later they do ease providing us with opportunities to look back and reflect on the lessons learned. The pressures, the circumstances we find ourselves in, are all part of the learning process in our spiritual unfoldment. Our soul never stops growing but it needs to continuously be tried and tested. This is how we learn; this is how we grow. The soul can never stand still; it must grow and evolve and it can only grow through the pains of birth, of well-tried and tested lessons.

We may sometimes feel we are failing. But what do we know of failure of the soul. How do we judge ourselves? Do we feel or think that the failures, as we believe them, of the outer personality reflect on the soul? It is the very aspiration, the very fear of failure that urges the soul to grow. We judge ourselves by our daily reactions to everyday life, to our everyday relationships and attitude to people. But how often are we told to stand back and judge from the eyes of spirit, not from the outer mind nor emotions. Sometimes we look at our successes deriving from meditation or spiritual endeavours. But the real successes are our daily struggles, our daily insecurities, our daily pains. For beneath all these struggles, all these pains and sufferings the soul is living, the soul is learning, the soul is endeavouring to penetrate through the pains of this birth of the Christ-child within each of us. How can you have a birth without the preceding pains? Does it not at times feel that it is never going to end? Have we ever wished that we could just give up there and then? At the moment of birth, the pain is at its most excruciating but it is after that we experience the feeling of joy and upliftment and look back at lessons well and truly learned. Will it not be worth the pain?

The birth of the Christ-child, the Christ-consciousness, the Light, is the same as the birth of a child. We need to go through these pains, these experiences to allow that beautiful Light to shine through and manifest itself in our lives. When fears and anxieties threaten to overwhelm us, keep on keeping on, striving ever forward, going through the pains, the difficulties, knowing that there is truly Light at the end of the tunnel. We need to gently persevere. We need to have faith and trust in our innermost being, who is guiding every step.

Perhaps every now and again, we need to reassess our lives, think on where we are, where we are going, what we are doing, what we are achieving within ourselves and without. Perhaps it is time to change a few things or conditions in our lives. It is often said, 'Change your thinking and you can change your life'. It is like having a good spring clean, a clearing out, a cleansing out. Things need to change. We cannot remain forever as we are. This is a natural progression of evolution. We need to change as individuals, as a nation and as a world. People change; places change; conditions change; and we need to change with them. It is when we refuse or ignore these changes that we suffer. Accept these changes for they are all part of growth. Not just our own growth but also the growth of humanity.

One of the greatest stumbling blocks of humanity is FEAR. Fear of rejection, fear of the future, fear of death, fear of illness, fear or insecurity, fear of criticism, fear of ridicule, and so on. So many different types of fear that affects us all, some are known, some are unknown. Sometimes, the further we go on the path, the more fears that will grip us. As the aspirant makes the soul contact, the soul then becomes more aware of the astral plane, and the surrounding astral influences which will affect him/her through others. There is great fear in the astral planes. The astral plane is one of emotion and fear is an emotion, although it can strongly affect the mind too. You are surrounded by the emotions of the people around you, the environment, the nation, the world, not forgetting racial or karmic influences. And as the aspirant progresses he or she becomes more sensitive to these conditions around and mistakenly thinks it is created by himself or herself. Very often we may find, when in a crowd situation, we will pick up the emotions or thought consciousness around us and mistake them for our own. We may feel depressed, or anxious, or fearful and believe it to be our own emotions or reactions. But this may not necessarily be so. It may be our sensitivity that is picking up all these emotions from those around us. It will be in the ether when we go to a large area of shopping or a theatre or any public place.

These feelings of depression, of failure, of anxiety etc. are not necessarily our own. When these feelings grip an aspirant on the path they become despondent and develop an inferiority complex. The aspirant may look around and see others so sure of themselves and their work. But what the aspirant fails to grasp is that it is by their very high level of attainment they have become more susceptible to the outside influences and therefore doubt their very own qualities, their very own achievements. The aspirant may fail to recognise the very wonderful qualities which they possess and which is being used to assist others. Because they stand as they ARE, in their very soul-deep humility, they cannot recognise what they ARE. Others may see them more clearly – but not themselves. They look at themselves from the outside, comparing themselves to others all the time, judging themselves as inadequate.

Unless we can stand back and recognise this we become submerged in the auric influences of emotions around us and think we are a failure. The astral plane is the closest to the earth planet and it is through the astral plane that the soul needs to penetrate to reach that beautiful light at the end of the tunnel. But it can easily be done right here and now. If we are aware of these astral influences around us and we define them for what they are – NOT OUR OWN – then we will find it easier to separate and disassociate ourselves from these feelings. We have our very own feelings and influences to recognise and get hold of – do not allow other influences to detract you from your pathway.

This does not mean that we cut ourselves off from people. Because it is only by being involved in life that we can evolve. We just need to understand and know ourselves so that we can detach ourselves from the astral influences around us. Let us go forward, be strong, let us not worry about making mistakes – it is the mistakes that will teach us the best lessons.

In time, we will get to grips with our own innermost feelings; our real soul feelings. It is like a nut that needs shelling, as we shell the layers the nut becomes clearer until we end up with only the inner food, the outer layers all shelled, all peeled off. Let us use the outer layers right now for our lessons, learn to recognise our lessons, be aware every moment of the day how each happening affects us, and see it for the opportunity it brings us to learn.

How do we walk the Spiritual Path?

Life itself, guided by our soul, with the impulse of spirit behind, will bring us the experiences that we need for our growth. It is important that we live the life that we have wheresoever we find ourselves. Each experience, each challenge is a stepping stone towards the ultimate goal, which is the full knowledge of ourselves as spirit. So, what are these stepping stones:

> An awakening – something starts shifting within
> An awareness – there is more to this life than I have been aware of before
> An acknowledgement – yes I am more than just my physical body
> A recognition – I can see; I can glimpse another aspect of myself
> Gnosis – yes now I know. Now I understand. I AM

To walk the spiritual path means acknowledging, accepting that there is more to you than just the physical. It means therefore that you acknowledge and accept others on earth as another soul journeying towards its own spiritual unfoldment. This brings us to the realisation how important it is not to judge or condemn others. If there is wrongdoing, judge or condemn the action, but not the individual soul for we truly do not know what lessons that soul is learning. It is so easy to jump to hasty conclusions and condemn.

Walking the spiritual path brings us the awareness, the knowledge that there are also other realms or kingdoms of which we may know very little about. Here I refer to the natural kingdoms such as the mineral, the vegetable and the animal kingdoms. As human beings, we have a responsibility to these other kingdoms. Then there is the awareness that there are other planets, other universes of which we know very little about.

We walk the spiritual path with the greater awareness that we are part of a greater life, a greater energy, a greater force than we could, with our finite minds, even possibly imagine. It is the awesomeness of nature, of the vastness of life around us that makes us truly humble. It can also inspire and encourage us to strive forward on that path.

How do we bridge the gap between life on earth and the world of spirit?

Probably the most difficult thing for humans to appreciate is that we are both divine and human. We have been indoctrinated for so many aeons of years to believe that we are born in sin and therefore not worthy to think anything of such exalting understanding or even aspiration. We bridge the gap by knowing who we are and by the understanding that we are innately divine and life on earth is a school for us to learn this. Through unfolding and developing our spiritual qualities we eventually come to the realisation of the two worlds being one. We are at the stage of development in humanity when we can grasp that we can only realise our divinity, understand our spirituality, by bringing this down into matter, into the physical.

It needs to be remembered that the world of spirit is within. This concept may be hard to grasp and it is humanly natural to look outside ourselves all the time for answers. And yet, those who practise meditation, know that what they can 'see', what they can 'visualise' is all within. So, perhaps it is not so difficult then to grasp that the world of spirit is reached by going within. All knowledge of other worlds is within. Where do you say? How do we find his? Remember that seed of creation. That seed holds all knowledge. So, it is in recognition and acknowledgment of the seed of creation within that we find other worlds.

The spirit, the very essence of our being, life itself, remains dormant but watchful. It allows the soul to gain experience of life but primarily the spirit acts as an impulse in the soul's journey leading it to eventual recognition of its true spiritual nature.

It is these experiences and the lessons that the soul learns from the successive lifetimes that bring the soul to its natural harvest. As the seasons unfold and grow, so does the soul and when it reaches the autumn of its path, it can look back, with the eyes of the spirit, and see what qualities have been unfolded and recognise who we are. Above all it has learned to balance the elements within so that the spirit, the life essence, is master.

What is there after this life on earth?

Life after death will depend on what we have put into this life by our thoughts, speech or actions.

At the time of the death of the physical body the cord (also known as the Silver Cord) which binds the physical to the etheric or vital body is cut by the Angel of death and then you are released into the world of your own making. The etheric or vital body is a replica of the physical body, the one great difference is that it does not have any physical disease or impediments.

Our awakening in the spiritual realms varies according to the awareness we may have acquired whilst on earth but each one will have a companion awaiting them. This may be a loved one who they immediately recognise or it could be a companion of old, who although not immediately recognisable will give you much support and help to make your transition easy and comfortable. Gradually as events unfold, we will come to recognise and know our companion of old.

If you have suffered great physical distress prior to your death, you will be taken to a healing environment, a healing chapel, where loving attendants, of both angelic and human forms will help your soul to recover from the distresses caused by your physical illness, or a sudden passing in peaceful and very beautiful surroundings.

You will never be left alone during this very important part of your transition and adjustment to the spiritual realms. If your passing was quick and free of long physical distress then you will be taken to a home which you will have built yourself by your earthly endeavours, and gradually a companion will show you around the spiritual realms. And you will also be amazed at the activity in the spiritual realms. There are Halls of Learning which include music, art, history, science, and many other forms of educational institutions. Nothing is compulsory. You choose what you want to do.

In the spiritual realms you will have the opportunities of doing or learning things which may not have been possible for you in your earthly life. (*I know that my own father is growing roses, we never had a garden on earth and he always wanted to grow flowers- well he is doing that now to his heart's content and many are the times when roses come to me and I know this comes from my Dad*). It may even be that you may wish to continue a particular study or project in which you have been very interested in and devoted much of your earthly life to. All things are possible if you have earned them. Although food or drink is not necessary in spirit, it is available until your desires for these things go.

There are many levels of consciousness in the spirit world and each one is attained by your own individual expansion and awareness. You carry on evolving in spirit, although there is no time there as is known on earth the soul does not stand still for long. After a time of relaxation, the spirit within, of its own accord, will realise there are other dimensions and will eventually want to know how to reach other heights and move on. Life is ever evolving, ever growing ever expanding.

The time will come when the soul, with the help of a guide or teacher, will face its own akashic record and will then understand where it is at in the path of evolution. It will then realise what else needs to be done for the unfoldment of the spiritual qualities and will then choose its path to enable this to happen.

The greatest journey we can ever take

The greatest journey that we can ever take is that which follows the path of the soul. We are very blessed to live in these times when awareness and participation in spiritual activities, other than the orthodox, is not punishable by torture. That said, there is today an abundance of information available which can be extremely confusing, especially for those souls become interested in spiritual matter for the first time, other than the orthodox. So what is the secret of finding the right path for ourselves? How can we steer a clear and direct course through the melee of confusion? I would say, we need to focus ourselves on the present moment and do what is in front of us – what we are being called to do right now. We need to remember that we are not on an ordinary journey where we have to prepare by looking up lots of information going hither and dither to buy this book or attending umpteen workshops and talks. The soul's journey does not need getting ourselves in a state about it, we do not have to rush anywhere to get information, and we do not need to buy anything nor to renew our passports or visas.

The soul's journey is one of inner exploration and excursion. The whole purpose of our lives is to discover who we really are. What is it that motivates us? The purpose of our life is part of the divine Plan. We are co-creators with the Divine. We have that inherent divinity within ourselves and our Earth journey is to help us to realise this. This journey is the outer manifestation of a soul exploration. Through countless lives, the soul proceeds to unfold and develop its spiritual qualities. These qualities are within us but they lie buried within our consciousness and it is the experiences of each lifetime that help us to unfold them. Slowly on this inner journey we realise the relationship between spirit, soul and body.

On this journey, we need no documents except what is true in our hearts. It is by our light that we are known. It is by our light that we are admitted into the realm of spirit. We need no outer clothing, no sun tan lotion, nor guide books to be admitted into the world of light. Our only passport is that of Love. It is by the love and light in our hearts that we gain admittance into the Kingdom of Heaven, the realm of the spirit. Only those who can see with the eyes of spirit can tell to what degree we have unfolded our spiritual qualities. But slowly as we begin to believe in ourselves, as we begin our own inner exploration, we will in time understand and know, truly know, who we are.

The map of the soul's path is all part of the Divine Plan. We have the blueprint; we just need to experience it.

……*and so it continues*

There is no beginning and no end to the spiritual path. It is simply a continuation of life, of existence from one plane to another. We do not lose who we are, our identity, it is merely merged into our greater self, our true spiritual essence. This spiritual essence, this energy, is part of an even greater Being. Compare it to a child growing up. A child goes to infant school, then junior school, then senior, college and possible university. Each step along the way is enriching that child with knowledge, each experience brings it more gifts, more skills. Some lessons are more difficult, perhaps even painful, than others. But nevertheless, all still valuable. Then we go through the school of life with all its challenges, all its ups and downs, all its many varied experiences, good and difficult. We can sometimes look back on our childhood experiences and reflect on how far we have come. We cannot undo the past but we can heal it, we can learn from all this and then move on.

We really do learn so much from the university of life. We may not attain degrees on the material level, but the soul has gathered the harvest of each experience. Nothing is wasted. The soul memory retains all and it is this memory that is manifested in our Akashic records. Every stepping stone along the way, every lesson learned is there for us to reflect upon, learn and move on.

The life of every human has an innate divinity. It is by going forward on the path of the soul that we both unfold and express this.

Be not afraid to take that step forward!
Use those stepping stones!

Printed in Great Britain
by Amazon